THE FOOTSTEPS OF OUR FATHERS

TALES OF LIFE IN NINETEENTH CENTURY ST. DAVID'S

PETER B. S. DAVIES

MERRIVALE

All rights reserved. No part of this publication may be reproduced, stored in a retrieval system or transmitted in any form or by any means electronic, mechanical, photocopying, recording or otherwise, without the prior permission of the author.

1. *Councillor Adrian Owen Williams in Court Dress on the occasion of the Coronation of George VI at which he represented, as Chairman, Pembrokeshire County Council: photograph dated 10 May, 1937.*

Copyright: Peter B. S. Davies 1994

ISBN 0 9515207 4 1

Acknowledgements

I wish to express my grateful thanks to the following institutions for allowing me to consult various documents in their possession and for the generous help and guidance provided by their staffs: National Library of Wales, Aberystwyth; Haverfordwest Record Office; Haverfordwest Reference Library; St. David's Cathedral Library.

I also wish to thank for permission to reproduce various illustrations in their possession: National Library of Wales, Aberystwyth, (Plates; 7, 14, 23, 24); Welsh Industrial & Maritime Museum, Cardiff, (16); Bristol Museum & Art Gallery, (34); Haverfordwest Record Office, (Newspaper cuttings and billheads); also Tabernacle Calvinistic Methodist Chapel, St. David's for permission to photograph the memorial to Herbert and Elizabeth Dixon and the painting of Rev. George Williams.

I am also grateful to those individuals who have kindly consented to lend me old photographs from their personal collections for reproduction in this volume: Prudence Bell, (39); Elwyn and Nancy Davies, (26, 27, 28, 31); Philip Dawson, (21, 37, 38); John Adrian Evans, (1); George Harries, (32); Mattie Stephens, (3) - and to Philip Clarke who made prints from the original Dawson collection.

In addition I wish to thank the members of the Williams family - past and present - and the many older inhabitants of St. David's for their memories of pre-war days in and around Old Cross: James Nicholas and Brinley Jenkins, whose fathers (George Nicholas and Ben Jenkins) were employed by Alderman Adrian Owen Williams; Tom and Barbara Spittle of Treleddyn; Mike Plant of Lower Treginnis; Dewi Rowlands (who worked at Treginnis for many years); Eunice Smith and Edna Morgan of Y Fagwr; Letitia Thomas; Mattie Stephens; Rosina Grey - all provided valuable information in a variety of ways; so too did Lilian Lloyd Jones - last surviving niece of Mr. Owen Williams - and her children, Lloyd and Jennifer, who succeeded him at Old Cross.

It is impossible to write about St. David's without being greatly indebted to David James who as always provided generous advice and assistance, particularly on the story of Dorothy Jordan and Treleddyn. Judith Disandolo kindly supplied me with much original research on the Tithe Map for which I am extremely grateful, as I am to Paul Raggett for his discovery of the photograph of the *Prince Cadwgan*. George Harries once more gave valuable and valued assistance in many respects. Finally I am particularly grateful to Prudence Bell who showed me and allowed me to quote from the personal diaries and letters of her great grandparents Herbert and Elizabeth Dixon; I sincerely hope that one day the full, tragic story of their martyrdom will be told by her; it is a story that deserves to be more widely known.

To My Parents

BRYN and MURIEL DAVIES

who, half a century ago, first aroused my interest in Local History and, in particular, the story of the Williams Family of St. David's.

2. *A family group c.1912 includes, on the left, the older children of Fred and Esther Sime; in rear Marion and John; in front Chrissie and Muriel. The two girls on the right are Tina and Jean Evans — 'Sime' cousins from Haverfordwest.*

Cover: Old Cross and Menai c.1945; photograph by W. Morris Mendus.

3. Adrian and Lilian Owen Williams in their younger days outside the front porch at Old Cross.

Contents

I	Tales from the Bank	7
II	Williams 'Old Shop'	14
III	A Royal Romance	22
IV	Invasion	27
V	Rock House	30
VI	A Mysterious Legacy	34
VII	Bristol Traders	38
VIII	A Financial Disaster	43
IX	A Liverpool Interlude	47
X	The Watts Harris Inheritance	50
XI	The Commercial and the Grove	57
XII	About the Cross	63
XIII	'Ratlin the Reefer'	74
XIV	Wreck of the *Prince Cadwgan*	79
XV	Tragedy at Treginnis	83
XVI	'Sion bob Ochr'	87
XVII	Martyrs of the Faith	91
XVIII	A Famous Rescue	96
	Genealogical Tables	101
	Bibliography	104

WILLIAMS FAMILY PROPERTY

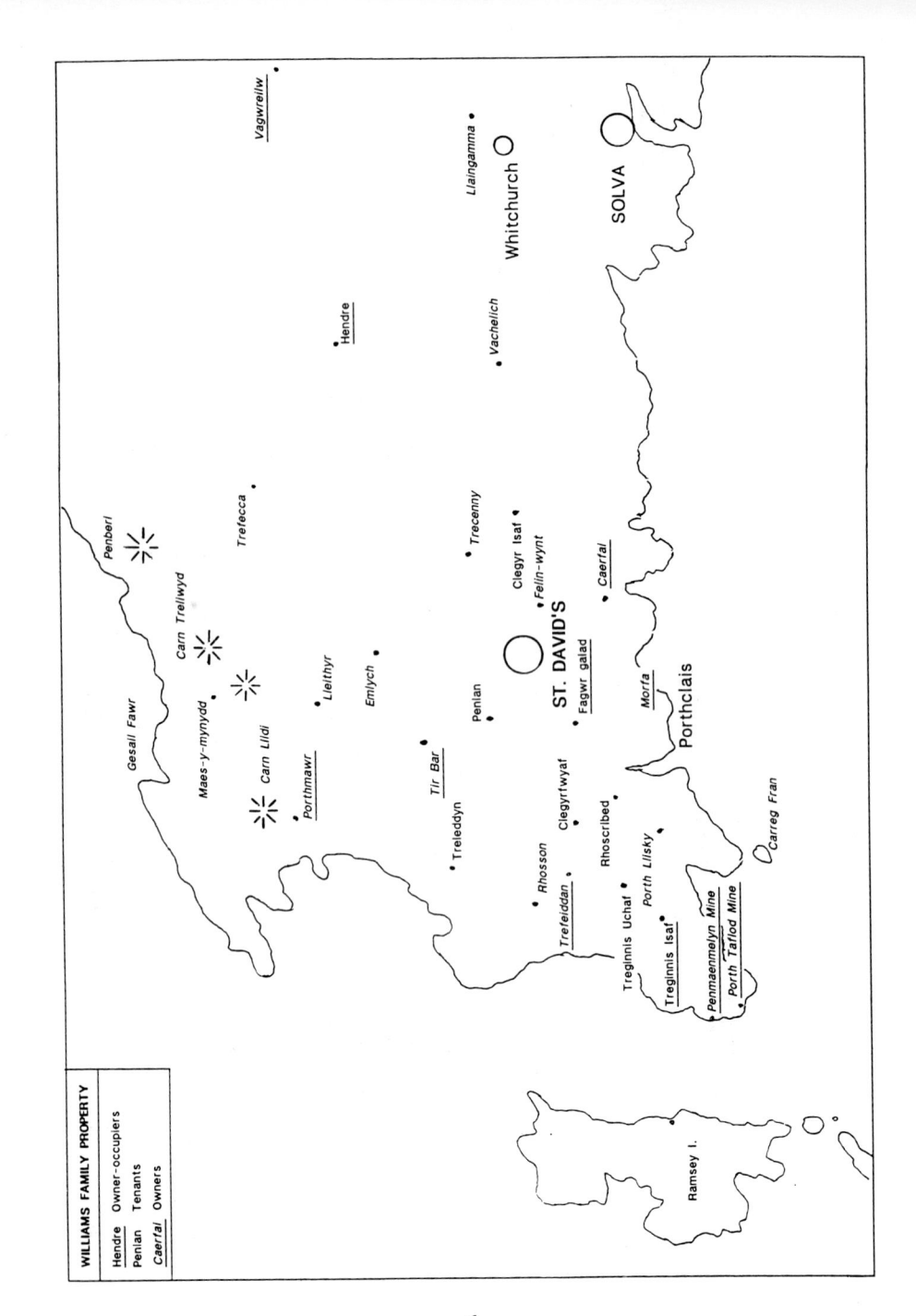

Hendre — Owner-occupiers
Penlan — Tenants
Caerfai — Owners

I; Tales from The Bank

To the younger members of the family who visited Alderman Adrian Owen Williams at Old Cross around the time of the Second World War it seemed that the room known as 'The Bank' had not changed in centuries, and probably never would. The dark, low, oak-beamed room was dominated by a massive, black-oak chest and a large iron safe on which newspapers and council documents were piled high. In the corner by the door stood a press. Above it hung a clock loudly ticking away the seconds; around its dial, in faded gold lettering, it bore the inscription "GOULDING'S MANURES". This room was where 'Uncle Owie' was almost invariably to be found when he was at home. The sitting room across the hall was used only on Sundays; the dining room at the rear with its long refectory table, by then, never.

Adrian Owen Williams had been born at Treginnis Isaf (Lower Treginnis) on 11th May, 1874. He was the only son and heir of George Owen Williams and his wife Mary Anne - formerly Bowen. From the farm the family had moved to the City Hotel and later to the Cross House Hotel - the present Menai. Mr. Owie Williams had been educated in St. David's and also at Aberystwyth University College where he studied agriculture, though he did not take a degree.

On the death of his mother in 1893, George Owen Williams had inherited a considerable estate located in the parishes of Hayscastle and St. Lawrence. It included the farms of Hayscastle, Trerhos, Tycant, Plaindealings, Plaindealings Fach and Penparc which had been created by the amalgamation of a number of smaller units once owned by Prebendary Watts Harris. After the death of his wife five years later he had retired from active life and handed over the estate to his son Adrian in exchange for an annuity.

About this time Adrian Owen Williams had married his first cousin Lilian Watts Williams, daughter of William Watts Williams, and they had taken up residence at Old Cross, then owned by Lilian's brother Samuel James Watts Williams. Adrian had taken over the business as general merchant which had previously been run by his father-in-law from Old Cross and, in order to expand, he had leased two of the granaries on the road to Porthclais.

He also owned premises in Lower Solva, near the Cambrian Inn, and he rented properties on the other side of the river, including stores and the limekiln near the Gamlyn, from Samson Thomas Williams of Tanyrallt. Mr. Owen Williams, who burned about 400 tons annually was one of the last of the lime burners in Pembrokeshire. Apart from the limestone and the culm to burn it he dealt in coal and in agricultural produce such as corn and butter and in superphosphate and other artificial fertilizers. Most of this was carried to the harbours of Solva and Porthclais in small coastal vessels like the *Mary Jane Lewis* whose master was William J. Lewis; the Williams family, once considerable shipowners, no longer owned any vessels.

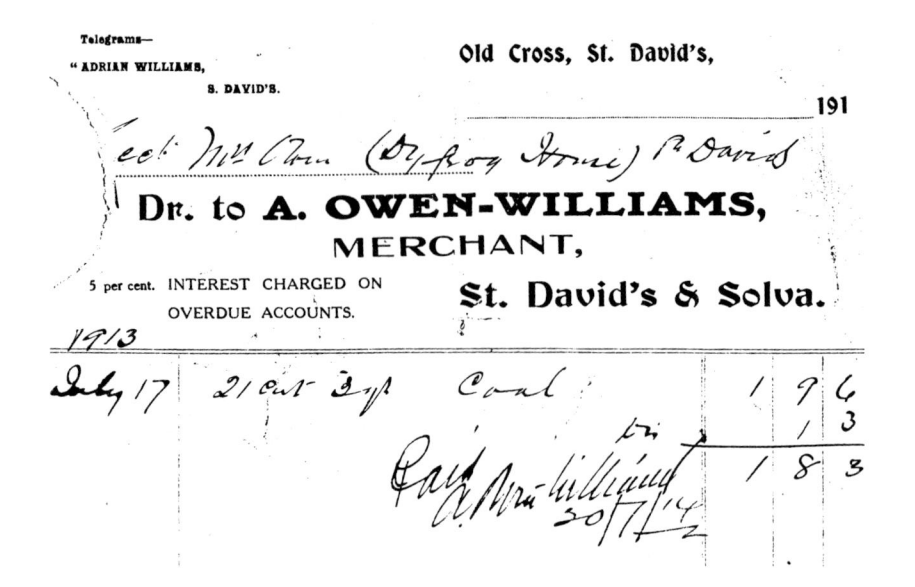

In his business Owie Williams was assisted by George Nicholas who had been brought up in the end cottage in the lane below the chemist's shop. He had started work with Mr. Williams when a young boy and by hard effort had achieved a position of responsibility. When Mr. Williams was elected to the County Council, George Nicholas, by then his right hand man, had become manager of the business. Eventually he ran the coal merchant operation on his own account.

It was in 1923 that Mr. Owen Williams first stood for the County Council. The election was held in the Council School where the count was to take place. In order to allay his wife's worries he arranged for a nephew-in-law to stand outside from where he could see into the room. It was decided that if he had won Mr. Williams was immediately to take a handkerchief from his pocket and mop his brow in a certain manner. The sign duly appeared and the messenger, Bryn Davies, was able to carry the good news to the anxiously waiting Mrs. Williams.

A large, dominating woman, invariably dressed in black, Lilian Owen Williams contrasted sharply with her husband. Fairly short, in later life stout, he was always to be seen about the streets smartly dressed in a grey suit with an immaculate bow-tie, his black shoes brightly polished, his tooth-brush moustache neatly trimmed and his greying hair brushed sprucely back. But Mrs. Owen Williams was herself a person of some consequence; she was, among other things, a Justice of the Peace who sat on the Dewisland Sessions which were held at the Courthouse at Mathry. Prominent in women's organisations, she was the first of her sex to speak publicly at the Temple of Peace in Cardiff.

For a quarter of a century Mr. Owen Williams represented the people of St. David's on the County Council. Painstaking and thorough, he served his constituents well; until his final illness, in all those years, he never missed a meeting of the council. He sat on over thirty sub-committees of the council and associated bodies including the South Wales Sea Fisheries Committee and the Welsh National Memorial Association, frequently travelling to places such as Cardiff, Aberystwyth and London at his own expense. In 1937 he was elected Chairman of the Pembrokeshire County Council and was its representative at the Coronation of King George VI. In 1941 he was appointed a Deputy Lieutenant for Pembrokeshire, and four years later he was raised to the aldermanic bench. Of him it was written:

"To all the affairs with which he was connected he brought cool, unruffled judgment, and he could always be depended upon to speak his mind no matter how unpopular were his views - and they were oftentimes unpopular. As a committee man, he could never be hurried or put off lightly, and he would always stick to his point if he considered it to be in the public interest."

In his native St. David's he was no less active. He acted as local agent for Lloyd's, he served on the Lifeboat Committee and was for forty years an active member of the local Lifesaving Association. Keenly interested in education he was a Governor at St. David's County (Grammar) School eventually becoming chairman. Whatever event took place in the locality, be it carnival, agricultural show or Solva Regatta, the unmistakable figure of Cllr. Owen Williams would be conspicuously present.

During the week scarcely a day would pass without his attending the Shire Hall in Haverfordwest in one capacity or another. Between meetings he and his cronies were generally to be found in the Dickensian tea rooms in Victoria Place which were kept by Miss Griffiths - a cheerless room notable for a crumbling artificial wedding cake and a faded railway map of Victorian vintage. Her currant buns were invariably dry and stale and the tea lukewarm and stewed. Miss Griffiths' establishment was an anachronism in the thriving county town. But there was an upstairs room where her favoured customers could meet in private to plan their strategies.

Sundays were different; no matter where he had been during the week he would attempt to be home by the weekend. He had been a member of Tabernacle all his life and was a regular member of the congregation. But it was the little Sunday School at Vachelich which was his greatest pride; he was the Superintendent, and hardly ever were he and his wife absent from its afternoon meeting. The annual tea-party at Vachelich was one of the most important events in his whole year.

In those days there were still few modern comforts in Old Cross. The Bank, with its roaring coal fire, was snug enough in the winter, but there was no electricity, and the equally large bedrooms could be icily-cold. There was no bathroom; water was drawn from a well behind the house, while lighting was by a flickering gas light or by oil lamps. In the outdoor 'Ty bach' squares torn neatly from the *Christian Herald* provided reading material for its occupants. The Owen Williamses did not own Old Cross; it had been the property of Lilian's brother Samuel Watts Williams, but was then owned by his widow Margaret. Adrian Owen Williams had no intention of spending money to improve a house which belonged to his sister-in-law: she in turn was not inclined to spend money for the rent she received.

Mrs. Watts Williams lived alone in the adjoining Menai, a much more modern house; her two children had moved away. In the New Crosses

4. The New Crosses; the nearer house became known as New Cross House, the further as New Cross.

10

lived two other cousins of Owie Williams, daughters of John Inkerman Williams. In the lower house - New Cross - was Miss Esther Williams, while next door in New Cross House lived her sister Lily, the wife of Capt. David Price.

There were other families who, like the Williamses, had lived on Cross Square at least from early Victorian days. Next door to New Cross was the butcher's shop of Gilbert Martin, whose family had lived there over a hundred years earlier when it had been a farm. The Gwalia was then a newsagents run by three spinster-sisters, the Misses Williams, granddaughters of William Williams who had been postmaster a century before. The Rees family of Belmont were descended from Martha Williams of the Commercial Inn who had purchased the site in 1837 from Harries of Priskilly.

The banks were comparatively new. Lloyds had taken over from the New Shop; Midland occupied London House; Barclays a purpose-built office on the corner of New Street. Morris Mendus, the chemist, lived directly opposite Old Cross in the shop which his predecessor Albert David had built on land purchased in 1891 from George Williams; the lower half of this was the Post Office, run by Mrs. Evans the widow of the previous chemist. The Beehive was an ironmongers, but during the war it was taken over as the headquarters of the local A.R.P. detachment.

But even at the end of the Second World War something of the old St. David's was still to be found on the square. At Gwalia the Misses Williams, hidden behind piles of newspapers, handed out the current issues as the waiting queues grew ever longer. The more impatient the visiting customer the longer they took, slowly counting out the change and exchanging local gossip with their friends. At Court House lived Miss Perkins - former infant teacher, Justice of the Peace, old-fashionedly forbidding in Bible-black, yet kindly - and her widowed sister Mrs. Lawrence. They ran a grocery store in the adjoining shop where the goods were laboriously measured out on old-fashioned scales. In Cartref Miss Smith ran a small one-roomed cafe and served cooked dinners to a few regular customers. Between Old Cross and Beehive was the old forge and ironmongers of the Roberts family. But they were a dying breed, the last of the old characters; soon all would be gone.

In their time Mr. and Mrs. Owen Williams had been great entertainers. Many came on business; tenants of the farms, dealers in corn, others to purchase culm and lime. There were other members of the County Council and those who came to consult their councillor. Visiting preachers at Tabernacle stayed at Old Cross and discussed religion and politics; Adrian Owen Williams was a staunch Liberal. When the Lloyd Georges visited St. David's (Gwilym, son of David, was the local Member of Parliament) they were feted at Old Cross. Relations from away came and stayed for much of the summer. Whoever called, visiting dignitary, or the humblest pensioner who came to the kitchen door, was made welcome.

Tradition was very important. Every child who called at Old Cross on New Year's Day was presented with a shiny new penny and an orange. Each of the poor was provided with a pat of butter, and tenants, calling to pay the rent, were given a meal; long established customs, these came to an end with rationing during the war.

In 1943 Mrs. Owen Williams died. Mrs. Brenda Morgan, who lived at the rear of Lloyds Bank and had worked for the family for many years, became housekeeper to Mr. Owen Williams. There was much less entertaining at Old Cross, but every evening when he was at home friends and relations would call and exchange gossip and reminisce about the olden days. There the younger members of the family heard for the first time tales of their ancestors.

Some of the stories were complete in themselves. George Owen Williams (Owie's father) had been keenly interested in photography, particularly that of nature. On one occasion he was engaged in this hobby somewhere near Milford. Without realising it he strayed into the military area around one of the forts and was arrested as a suspected spy. He was kept in custody overnight before he was able to establish his innocence.

Most of the tales were more involved. The family had lived on Cross Square for about a century. Originally they had been farmers, the Williamses and the families into which they had married; Williams and Harries at Treginnis, Bowen at Treleddyn, Harris at Hendre, Watts at Hayscastle. Each farm had its stories. Treginnis had its tale of the old copper mine on Ramsey Sound and the tragic accident which led to its closure; it had also the tale of the shipwreck of the *Prince Cadwgan* on Carreg Fran and of how the farmer was marooned on the island - and of the strange twist of fate that followed half a century later. At Treleddyn there was the story of how the Duke of Clarence came to visit his actress friend at the big house of Treleddyn Uchaf and of the ceiling there with its royal decoration.

The Williamses had eventually left the land to become shopkeepers; from the Old Shop in Nun Street they had expanded and become merchants and shipowners and had settled at Rock House (Y Fagwr). They had moved for a time to Cardiff and later to Liverpool where they had become ship-brokers. They had made money and they had lost money - some of it in shipping, but largely at the hands of lawyers for whom there was a deep distrust in the family.

A niece of Owie Williams, Christina Sime - one of six attractive, though very different sisters - had a boy friend who was studying the law. She had been brought up in the family tradition and one day, half jokingly, said to him that lawyers never went to Heaven. The remark was taken to heart and it was the end of a beautiful friendship.

In 1862 the family had returned from Liverpool. Owie's grandfather Samuel Williams had married Elizabeth Owen of Hendre, the daughter of a sea captain. Her uncle, Prebendary William Watts Harries of Haverfordwest, had left her his considerable estates, and they were able to live in comfort largely on the rents of their properties. But they could not be idle; there were forays into hotel-keeping and farming. Not all the family could stay at home; several went to sea and became master mariners - one at least was a Cape Horner in the days of sail. One of the nieces became a missionary and died a horrible death during the Boxer Rebellion in China.

These were some of the tales that were told by the fireside in the Bank by the patriarch of the Williamses. His younger relations listened fascinated if at times uncomprehendingly. The stories belonged to a world they had never known. When they were older they would understand. But on Monday, 12th January, 1948, 'Uncle Owie' died. He left no children, he was the last of his line. There would be no more tales.

5. Old Cross as it was around the time of the Second World War.

II; Williams 'Old Shop'

The day after the fire in 1784 (or was it 1785) which totally destroyed it, the farm at Upper Treginnis presented a scene of desolation. Now roofless, its timbers charred, its once-white walls soot-blackened, it had been home to Henry and Anne Williams and their family. By the time the flames had reached the thatched roof there had been no hope of saving the house or the attached farm buildings. The family could only watch helplessly as their home and its contents were consumed by the flames.

To Henry's widowed mother, who lived with them, it was particularly sad. As Elizabeth Rees she had been born at Upper Treginnis over seventy years earlier. In 1737 she had married George, eldest surviving son of Francis and Elizabeth Williams of Clegyrfwyaf. Two years later Francis and George Williams had obtained a lease of Rhoscribed for the lives of George, his wife and his younger brother Thomas. Tragically George died in 1741 when he was only 35 years of age.

It was his brother Thomas who benefited by George's death. He, not George's widow, succeeded to the tenancy of Rhoscribed; his descendants were still there over a century later. Disillusioned, in effect disinherited, Elizabeth returned with her two small children to her old home. She never forgave her in-laws and the name Francis does not appear again in the Treginnis family.

Henry had married Anne Harries from nearby Lower Treginnis and had eventually taken over the tenancy of Upper Treginnis. They had worked hard, and had made it into one of the most prosperous farms in the area. Now all that was gone. They and their five children - William, the eldest, was aged about fifteen and Phebe, the youngest, only a baby - were homeless.

Devastated by the loss of their livelihood, Henry and Anne Williams decided to give up farming. They moved into St. David's, to a house in Nun Street, not far from the square. Here, to provide for their young family they opened a shop. From these small beginnings was to develop the leading merchant business in the city.

To George, six years of age and youngest of their four sons, the change was equally traumatic. He had exchanged the freedom of living on a farm for what must have seemed to him the restrictions of street life in an urban community. And, perhaps more significantly, he had to go to school.

He did not take kindly at first to the discipline at the school of which Mr. John Jenkins was master. One afternoon George and some of his friends decided to play truant. Initial excitement changed to fear as he anticipated the wrath which was about to descend upon him. Henry

6. *The old round-chimneyed farmhouse of Clegyrfwyaf, as drawn by Romilly Allen in 1883. During the 1720s Francis Williams was tenant of Clegyrfwyaf; in 1704 Henry Williams (presumably his father) lived there.*

Williams was renowned for his fiery temper and expected obedience from his children at all times.

George did not return home that evening and was found only after a lengthy search. Retribution was swift and decisive! He was removed from the school and transferred to the Cathedral Grammar School where Rev. John Jones was master. He had found his ideal mentor. At his new school, which was held in the old Chapter House that then stood to the west of the cathedral, he became an outstanding student. He had learned his lesson; never again was he tempted to play truant.

The next escapade in which George was involved was much more serious. On Wednesday, 22nd February, 1797, the French landed near Fishguard. To George and his friends here was an opportunity for adventure. His experiences were afterwards recounted to his children and, nearly a century later, recorded in a letter written by his son George Williams of Llysyfran and reprinted in *Pembrokeshire Antiquities*.

"The day before the French landing at Strumble Head, the French ships had been sighted off St. David's Head, going quietly up channel and bearing ominously towards land. A gentleman then living at Trelethyn of the name of Williams, well acquainted with shipping, knowing well the rig of all craft passing, gave out the report that the French had certainly come. The result of this was that throughout the whole neighbourhood of St. David's men put their heads together as

7. *A view, dated 1806, of St. David's from a point near the Castell. The identity of the artist is uncertain.*

to the best means of preparation for the enemy. A number of young men - my father among them - having obtained a quantity of lead from the Cathedral, spent the best part of the night at the smithy casting bullets. As soon as they heard that the French had landed they started off with their smooth bores, and other preparations for the field of battle, thus greatly adding to the anxiety of those they left at home. My father was away two days, a lad not yet nineteen, and when his brother was sent in search, he found him with five or six others leading a number of French prisoners towards Haverfordwest.

"He was prevailed upon to return to his parents who were in such trouble on his account, and the others proceeded with the prisoners, who were, of course, disarmed and going quietly along."

For the second time George returned home in a somewhat chastened mood. But it was no longer a happy home. About this time his brother John had, after hearing some of the sermons of visiting preachers, become a Presbyterian Methodist; soon afterwards he was joined by his mother. George, still at school and intending to become a minister in the Established Church, like his father remained true to the old faith. A deep rift developed between the two factions, and George quarreled violently with his brother.

The families of both Henry and Anne Williams had close connections with the cathedral and its ministry which stretched back for many

8. *The domestic portion of Old Shop has probably not changed greatly since Victorian days. The shop itself, on the left, has been virtually completely rebuilt.*

generations. All had worshipped there; most had been baptised, married and buried there. Among the vicars choral - part-time farmers, part-time clerics who served the cathedral - were Thomas Harries of Lower Treginnis, appointed lay vicar choral in 1702, and Henry Williams who became vicar choral and organist in 1727. They were respectively great grandfather and great uncle of the young George.

However, within a year George had fallen under the spell of the itinerant preachers. Despite his father's admonition that he "might as well become a tinker if he left the Established Church", George had left school and joined the Methodists in their New Street Chapel.

Conditions at home had become unbearable, and George decided he must leave; but there was no opening available. Then, at last, he was offered the opportunity of travelling to India to take up the position of personal secretary to a gentleman in that distant land. To accept meant leaving Britain - probably for ever. But his mind was made up. He would go.

Preparations were complete; his passage was booked, and he was on the point of leaving. He came home to St. David's to say his farewells to family and friends. On the Sunday before he was due to sail he made, as he thought, one final visit to the chapel in New Street to listen to the last sermon in the Welsh language he would ever hear. The preacher was Mr.

Robert Dafydd from Caernarvonshire; his text was from the Book of Ruth. Little did the minister think of the effect his words would have on one young man in the congregation.

The passage was that in which Naomi begs Ruth: "Stay!". To George it seemed that the message was directed to him personally. He changed his mind and decided to remain in his native Wales.

The tensions in the home were as bad as ever; he could not live in the same house as his parents. At length, through the good offices of a visiting minister, George was persuaded to take up a post as master of a school in Newcastle Emlyn. It was a task for which he was ideally suited. Two happy and successful years followed before ill-health struck and he was forced to give up teaching, to the regret of parents and children alike.

For a year he worked for one of the chief traders of the town, before moving to the much larger town of Carmarthen to take up a similar post which offered a better salary. Here was the society he sought; men like Rev. David Charles; men of education who enjoyed religious debates and discussions in the Welsh language. And here he might have remained, for this was to prove the happiest period of his life.

Then, on 16th September, 1804, his mother died. Anne Williams had been the real driving force behind the enterprise; her husband was no real businessman. The older sons were all settled; William had married Elizabeth Williams of Penlan, and had succeeded to the tenancy of the farm; John became a farmer at Lower Clegyr. Thomas, later innkeeper of the Commercial Inn in High Street, was at this time a carpenter and cabinet maker. None wished to take over the shop.

There remained George; his relations implored him to return to run Old Shop. It must have been a difficult decision for him to make. St. David's could not compete with Carmarthen, then one of the largest towns in Wales, in terms of commerce. But at least he would be his own master.

In the end he accepted the challenge. He became reconciled with his father, although the latter remained in the Established Church, and they lived together at Old Shop until Henry's death twelve years later.

The shop which Anne Williams opened and operated for two decades never amounted to anything more than a village store. Her son, however, proved to be an astute man of business. Armed with the experience he had gained elsewhere and aided by his wife Elizabeth, whom he had married in 1810, he expanded it greatly. Grocer, draper, tallow chandler, ironmonger, and much besides, George Williams became the dominant trader in the city.

But his influence extended far beyond Old Shop itself. In 1819 he obtained a lease of the windmill at Twr y felin. He became a merchant dealing in corn and butter. It started in a small way; farmers would barter their produce against goods purchased in the shop. To store the corn Mr. Williams acquired the two lower granaries which stand beside the road to the harbour. He became a lime burner at Porthclais; he did much to improve the harbour where much of the trade was his, and he owned several of the boats which carried that trade.

Successful in business, devoted to his family, Mr. Williams became a respected deacon and was largely responsible for constructing a new and larger chapel in Goat Street, the original Tabernacle. Essentially a self-made man, in his later days he must often have recalled that awful day, half a century earlier, when he had gazed on the smouldering embers of his boyhood home. And given thanks for all the blessings he had received.

It was the custom for visiting preachers to be entertained at Old Shop. After supper Mr. Williams would settle down with the visitors in the dimly-lit, oak-beamed living room to discuss and argue about religious topics, often until the early hours. But, whether visitors were present or not, it was the tradition for family prayers to be said before the children retired to bed. However, on one occasion so engrossed did the group become in the discussions that prayers were totally forgotten. During the night the wind rose to a severe storm which blew down the sails from the windmill and severely damaged the tower. George Williams ever afterwards attributed the disaster to his neglect of family prayers. It was an omission that was never repeated.

In his spare time Mr. Williams would often wander on his own around the countryside. He invariably carried his Bible - always his favourite reading matter - and would seek some sheltered spot where he could study a portion of the scriptures. As he grew older he found he could not walk far without becoming tired and he developed a raging thirst which he could not quench. He became ever more frail until he needed assistance to attend chapel; eventually he was confined to his bed. On 3rd November, 1838, he died.

It was on his widow Elizabeth that the burden of running Old Shop and his other ventures fell. Ebenezer, the eldest son, was already married, the others had not yet completed their education. For some years it meant that Elizabeth Williams had to carry on alone. Later Ebenezer set up on his own account as a druggist on the square while Samuel took over the merchant and shipping aspects of the business. It was George, youngest of the three brothers, who inherited the Old Shop itself.

It was not his chosen career. Like his father before him, the young George had intended to become a Minister of the Gospel, though in his case it was as a Presbyterian Methodist. He had studied at at Bala and

9. *Rev. George Williams of Llysyfran, former minister at Tabernacle - from a portrait in the vestry of Tabernacle Chapel.*

later at Trefecca, where he was the first student to enrol at the college. But, after completing his education and qualifying for the ministry, he had, like his father, to come home to St. David's to manage the Old Shop.

He had married Eliza, daughter of Rev. William Morris the greatly respected minister at Tabernacle who lived in Bryn Siriol (Mount Pleasant) at the end of Mitre Lane. By 1851 the family had settled at Old Shop. Unlike the shop where his father began, the business which he inherited was large and flourishing; the young George Williams was grocer, linen and woollen draper, silk mercer, hosier and haberdasher as well as tallow chandler. In addition he dealt in ironmongery and funeral furnishings. Like his father before him he bartered butter and cheese for the goods which he sold.

George Williams and the Old Shop survived the problems which afflicted the Williams family during the 1850s. But his days as a shopkeeper were coming to their end. In 1861 he still lived at the premises with his wife and eleven year old daughter - but he was now also minister of Tabernacle. His father-in-law had died earlier in the year and George Williams had been appointed in his place. Later that same year his wife died and the new minister gave up his business.

So ended the association of the Williams family with the Old Shop, an association which lasted for three generations and almost eighty years. Rev. Williams moved with his young daughter to Bryn Siriol, the home of his mother-in-law. He devoted himself to his position as minister and saw to the building of the new Tabernacle, the much larger and more ornate chapel on the site of its precursor. His daughter Mary Anne married W. D. Williams of Gwalia but tragically she died in 1877, the year which saw the opening of the new chapel.

Devastated at his loss George Williams was a few years later offered the opportunity of taking up the ministry at Gwastad, near Llysyfran, his mother's old home. He married again and lived there, revered and respected, for some thirty years until his death in 1912 at the ripe old age of 92 years.

The career of George Williams of Llysyfran, as he is usually remembered, culminated in his being appointed to the position of Moderator of the General Assembly of the Presbyterian Church of Wales. It was something of which his father, who never achieved his own ambition, would have been justly proud.

And Old Shop, more than two centuries after Henry and Anne Williams began it, still houses a grocery store.

Saint Davids March. 1856.

Mrs Martins, Jewelly.

Bot of George Williams

Linen & Woollen Draper

Silk Mercer, Hosier & Haberdasher

TALLOW CHANDLER &C.

Funerals Completely Furnished.

1856.

1 Blk Satin Hdkf 5/. 1 Blk Silk 4/6 t — 9 6.
1 Satin Tie 3/. 3 Gents Rid 2/. — 9 —

III; A Royal Romance

Once upon a time there was a royal prince, heir to the throne, who fell in love with one of the leading actresses of the day. It is a story which has all the ingredients of a romantic novel, but it is a true story. The prince was the Duke of Clarence who later became William IV; the actress Dorothy Jordan; and there was a St. David's connection.

The link was with Treleddyn, more particularly with Upper Treleddyn, the solid Georgian farmhouse with its royally decorated ceiling. In the late eighteenth century it was the home of Thomas Williams - a remarkable man; one-time sailor, owner of several ships, agent for the Smalls lighthouse, owner of lead mines at St. Elvis and coal mines near Newgale, and once High Sheriff for Pembrokeshire. But it is as the man who gave the first warning of the French invasion in 1797 that he is best remembered.

His first wife was equally remarkable. Born Blanch Scudamor Phillips, youngest daughter of Thomas Phillips of Treleddyn, she inherited all his considerable estates as all her brothers and sisters predeceased her. Having been brought up at Treleddyn, Blanch had a keen interest in the sea. From the house, the North Bishop is clearly visible, and one day about 1780 she caught sight of some tiny figures clinging to one of the lesser rocks in the group. Her husband was away from home, and without hesitation Blanch launched a small boat from the creek beneath the house and battled her way across the foaming waters to the rock.

Landing on these exposed rocks is difficult and dangerous at the best of times, but in the stormy conditions prevailing it must have been next to impossible. But Blanch had sailed these waters since a child, and against all the odds she succeeded in taking aboard the seven survivors of a wrecked Swedish vessel who had all but given themselves up for lost. Then began the equally hazardous passage of the heavily laden boat back to shore. Finally, this local Grace Darling provided food and shelter for the shipwrecked mariners at her home in Treleddyn.

The house at Upper Treleddyn had at least one unusual feature apart from its famous ceiling. From one of its cellars a tunnel ran to the shore at nearby Porth Sele. The cellar opening has been bricked up and the seaward end is blocked by a cliff fall, though part was open in living memory. The local tradition is that it was once a tunnel used by smugglers. Thomas Williams may have been a magistrate, but it was not unknown for such men to be among the gentlemen who rode by silently at night. If it had been discovered he would probably have claimed it was only a level dug, like others nearby, in search of copper.

Blanch died in 1786, and Thomas later remarried, his second wife being Margaretta Theodosia Harries from Tresissyllt. Thomas and his

10. Upper Treleddyn, home of the Blands. Their sister, the actress Dorothy Jordan, often visited here in the company of the Duke of Clarence.

wife were not the only inhabitants of Upper Treleddyn, the other occupants were Nathaniel Bland and his sister Hester. Nathaniel acted as gamekeeper on the estate, but the Blands were no mere servants.

In his will Thomas Williams left Treleddyn to the Blands according to the wishes of his late wife. Who were they that they should be the beneficiaries of Blanch's will? They were not her siblings, nor were they her nephew and niece. Almost certainly they were - as suggested by David W. James - the children of her first cousin Grace Phillips. Certainly they were near relations, as Blanch and Lucy (another sister of Nathaniel Bland) are buried together by the south wall of the churchyard.

There was a third Bland sister who sometimes came to Treleddyn; on occasion she was visited there by her gentleman friend. The name Dorothy Bland is long forgotten; but by her stage name of Dorothy Jordan she became famous. Like her mother and her aunt before her, Dorothy became an actress.

Grace and Mary were two of the three daughters of George Phillips who, it is said, was a clergyman residing in Haverfordwest. The two sisters had run away from home, apparently to go on the stage. They played in touring companies and somewhere Grace met, and later married, Francis Bland. Her husband was the disinherited son of Nathaniel Bland, a Dublin judge. Described variously as an actor and a soldier -

he took the title of 'Captain' - he was something of a ne'er-do-well, which perhaps explains why some of the children came to live at Treleddyn.

The eldest of the children was Hester; the second Dorothy, who was born in London on 21st November, 1761, and baptised at St. Martin in the Fields a fortnight later. Francis eventually deserted his wife and children, and Grace was forced to return to the stage. It was in Ireland that Dorothy had her first experience of acting, after which she and her mother and aunt appeared in a company which toured in Scotland and the North of England.

Her mother and aunt spent the rest of their lives with the company, but Dorothy was destined for greater roles. During the late 1780s she came to London to act at Drury Lane. Here she became the mistress of Sir Richard Ford, part owner of the theatre, a liaison which produced three children. Soon Dorothy Jordan was the greatest comedy actress of her day, acclaimed by all the critics who flocked to see her.

It was hardly surprising that William, Duke of Clarence, should visit the theatre to see the actress whose smile (according to the critics) had the effect of sunshine and who could make even Methodists laugh. Like the critics the Duke was captivated by her charms and they became lovers.

Her older sister Hester was entrusted with the care of the children of Dorothy and Sir Richard Ford. Soon the Duke of Clarence and Dorothy Jordan were living together in the Duke's apartments as man and wife, though Dorothy did not entirely forsake the stage. In all they lived together for twenty years, during which time she bore him ten children who took the name of Fitzclarence. The couple were to all intents and purposes man and wife, and were regarded as such. Their children were accepted by society; only the orthodoxy of Church and State prevented their union from being made legal.

Mrs. Jordan - as she was known on the stage - never forgot her Pembrokeshire roots and her relations in St. David's; some at least of the Blands had settled at Treleddyn by the mid-1770s, when 'Aunt Blanch' was in possession. From time to time the Blands were visited there by their famous actress sister. Her arrival was the occasion for much celebration and Major Harries of Trevaccoon was accustomed to sending his carriage to Treleddyn for her personal use.

By the time Dorothy first met the Duke, Blanch was already dead; soon afterwards Thomas Williams married again. But Dorothy continued to visit her brother and sister in St. David's. After all Treleddyn had belonged to Blanch; her husband was effectively tenant for life, and Nathaniel and Hester would eventually inherit the property. Perhaps Dorothy saw in Treleddyn a haven should events go wrong.

The Duke apparently came to visit his mistress at Treleddyn on a number of occasions. Tradition says he used to come by sea, disembark at Whitesands, and ride on horseback across the dunes to the house. On one occasion at least he came to Haverfordwest and stayed awhile at the Castle Hotel. But usually it was in the big house at Treleddyn that he made his quarters.

The comings and goings at Upper Treleddyn would have been noted with interest at the farmhouse of Lower Treleddyn - the two houses stand cheek by jowl. The tenants at Lower Treleddyn in 1790 were Thomas and Mary Bowen; their descendants continued to farm there for much of the following century. The Blands however died out with Nathaniel and Hester, and the big house passed into other hands. It was left to the Bowens to pass on the tradition of the royal visitor to later generations.

In 1864 Mary Anne Bowen, granddaughter of Thomas and Mary Bowen, married George Owen Williams. Their daughter Esther was born at Lower Treleddyn two years later; their son Adrian Owen Williams at Lower Treginnis in 1874. So it transpired that, a century and a half after the events had taken place, Old Cross was among the few places where the story was remembered.

Over the years many of the details had been forgotten. But the essentials remained; the famous actress who came to stay with her

11. *The partly obscured memorial to Blanch Scudamor Williams and her Bland relatives in the south wall of the cathedral burial ground.*

relatives, the royal personage who visited her there, and the ceiling that was carved over their bed. As far as is known, none of their children was born at Treleddyn; but perhaps it was there, beneath the Royal Arms, that some of them began their entry into the world.

There was to be no happy ending to the story, affairs of state could not permit it. The visits to Treleddyn ceased, eventually the couple parted. Her career as an actress over, Dorothy fled, not to Treleddyn, but to Paris where she lived in poverty and seclusion. And there, in 1816, she died and was buried at St. Cloud, not as Dorothy Jordan, but as Mrs. James. Strangely, Pembrokeshire's other and better known royal mistress, Lucy Walter of Roch, also died in penury in Paris a century and a half earlier.

The grave in which the once-famous actress was buried has long since vanished; so too has the decorated ceiling at Treleddyn, in the room which she once shared with the future king. But Nathaniel, her brother, and Hester and Lucy, her sisters, lie in the shadow of the Close Wall; so too does her 'Aunt Blanch'.

What precisely was the relationship between Blanch Scudamor Williams and the Blands? Blanch's missing will - if it could be found - might tell us. Thomas Bowen certainly knew, but it was a detail he, or his successors, did not pass on. It does not affect the essentials of the story, indeed the air of mystery adds to its fascination.

William IV never produced a legitimate heir. Had events turned out differently, perhaps a Fitzclarence, and not Victoria, would have succeeded to the throne of Britain.

IV; Invasion

It was the custom of John Roach, when the normal day's work was done, to take a look round part of his extensive farm at Lleithyr. Most of his land lay on the southern side of the range of hills north of St. David's - but this evening he had elected to visit some of his fields near Maes-y-mynydd, an isolated hamlet north of the hills, huddled beneath the crest of Carn Treliwyd.

As he descended the slopes towards the shore he became aware of figures moving on the cliffs below him. In this remote spot he would not have expected to see anyone, and he decided to investigate. He made his way cautiously towards the little creek of Gesail Fawr at the foot of Carnllidi. Whoever the strangers were they had no business to be there.

As he came nearer, through the gathering gloom he caught sight of the masts of several vessels lying in the normally deserted inlet, and he could hear the splashing of oars as small boats made their way towards the shore. By this time he could hear the muffled sound of voices, but he could not make out what they were saying; to him they seemed to be speaking in a foreign language.

It was the year 1797. There could be only one explanation. They must be French troops bent on invasion. As rapidly as he could, without drawing their attention, Mr. Roach made his way back to the farm. Pausing only to warn his servants to round up all the stock and drive them to safety, he hurried on to St. David's to raise the alarm.

John Roach must have thought of the events which had taken place earlier that year. On Wednesday, 23rd February, Thomas Williams of Treleddyn had seen four ships which he as an old sailor had recognised as French men-of-war sailing northwards along the coast. Mr. Williams had sent a farm servant to carry the news to St. David's, while he had followed the ships along the coast.

Obviously, the first essential - as on the previous occasion - was to inform the civil and military authorities in Haverfordwest. A swift horse was required, and the swiftest available was a mare belonging to Rev. Arthur Richardson, organist of the cathedral. Horse and rider set off through the darkness, as though their lives depended upon it, up hill and down dale, the sixteen miles - and as many hills - to the county town. According to legend, the journey took just forty minutes, and when they reached Haverfordwest the gallant mare fell - never to rise again.

Meanwhile, back in St. David's, plans were hurriedly drawn up to meet the threat. There were no regular forces based in the locality; the citizens would have to cope as best they could until help arrived. But, with the enemy only two miles away, that help would almost certainly arrive too late.

There were, it is true, in both Solva and St. David's a handful of 'veterans' of the Fishguard campaign. In the few months since then they had doubtless regaled their elders - and particularly the young ladies - with tales of their exploits. Now the courage of these heroes would once more be put to the test. It was hardly a pleasant prospect.

The young men of St. David's - some like George Williams were mere schoolboys - had been extremely fortunate on the previous occasion. By the time they had collected sufficient weapons and ammunition and had reached Pencaer, the enemy had surrendered. Some had not even got that far. Against regular troops, these untrained and ill-equipped amateurs would have stood no chance.

The sailors from Solva were slightly better prepared. They had been led by Henry Whitesides, a native of Liverpool, who had designed and built the Smalls lighthouse; he had married the daughter of the Ship Inn and had settled in Solva. The small party had engaged the enemy in a skirmish, and had actually killed one of the Frenchmen. Few of the military could claim as much, and their success must have been much celebrated in the Ship.

A handful of inexperienced volunteers was all that stood between the enemy and St. David's. And surely the enemy was better prepared than on the previous occasion. The locals had heard the tales of rape and pillage, even of murder, that befell the inhabitants of Pencaer. This time it would be the denizens of Solva and St. David's who would suffer, and the cathedral that would be desecrated.

While some began to remove the treasures of the cathedral to safety, others set out to reconnoitre the positions which the French had taken up. To their surprise they found no troops massed on the cliffs. There were ships, but they were only coastal craft, becalmed by lack of wind, waiting for the tide to turn. The 'invaders' were simply seamen who had taken the opportunity of coming on shore to replenish their casks with fresh water.

The reconnaissance party, greatly relieved, hurried back to St. David's with the news that the citizens could, after all, sleep soundly in their beds that night. Another messenger was despatched post haste to Haverfordwest with the good tidings. But it was too late! Already news of the invasion had been spread around the county. The whole of Pembrokeshire and beyond was in a state of confusion.

One man perhaps had mixed feelings about the revelations of the scouting party; John Roach who had caused the alarm to be raised in the first instance. It was some time before orders for mobilization could be countermanded, and the cost was considerable. It was much longer before the civilian population returned to normal, and all because of a disastrous mistake made by one man.

Poor John Roach must have cursed the evil chance that took him to Gesail Fawr that evening. If only there had been enough wind for the ships to continue their voyages. If only he had checked more carefully before jumping to conclusions. If only ...... ! Instead of being a hero, he was a laughing stock, in danger of prosecution. Fortunately for him, the authorities were understanding, and accepted that his subsequent actions showed it was an error made in good faith.

Far less forgiving were the folk of St. David's. Because of him they had been greatly inconvenienced and severely frightened. It was a long time before they began to see the amusing side of the incident. For many a long year afterwards tales were told in the Black Lion and in cottage parlours, not only of 'French Pencaer', but also of 'French Roach Lleithyr'. John Roach never did entirely live down his mistake.

12. Gesail Fawr, where John Roach mistakenly thought the French had landed.

V; Rock House

"Late spring is delightful at St. David's, with the fresh green covering all, and the glorious gorse in full bloom all along the cliffs, while the clear blue sky rivals the blue ocean beneath. But early summer must be even more delightful. The tourists crowd to St. David's in August only. At other times the visitor has it nearly, if not quite, to himself. .... The ambitious climber may find several new routes (other than the usual one from the west) up the height of Carn Llidi, which towers up 592ft. above the level of the sea and commands a most superb view of the promontory of Dewisland and of the ocean which surrounds it."

So wrote Rev. W. A. B. Coolidge, Tutor in English History at Magdalen College, Oxford, in 1888. An American by birth, distantly related to President Coolidge, he was considered by many to be the outstanding Alpine climber of his time. He came many times to St. David's, usually to the Cross House Hotel, and each time he stayed longer than before. Whole families came, well-to-do families like Richards of Cardiff and Rees of Newport. They took over large houses completely, they brought their own servants, and they stayed for months.

One of these houses was Y Fagwr, then known as Rock House. At the end of the Victorian era it was owned by Mr. Tregarmer Rees of Newport, Gwent. According to John Miles Thomas, in his evocative account of life in St. David's at the time, the house stood empty for most of the winter. But during the summer it was occupied by the family with their grown up children and their friends. Those were the days; tennis on the lawn, rides on the ponies which were kept in the paddock, day-long visits to Whitesands in a pony cart, lavish picnics on the beach. Occasionally, a few, a privileged few, of the local children were invited to join in the festivities, but most could only gaze in wonder from afar.

The First World War ended all that. Y Fagwr became the home of the well known auctioneer Herbert Nathanael Jones and his family. After the Second World War it was bought by a grocer, John Smith, whose business premises were, by a quirk of fate, Old Shop in Nun Street. His wife, formerly Eunice Morgan of Porthclais, ran Y Fagwr as a guest house. But it could never recapture the gaiety of those Edwardian days.

A description of Rock House is given in the *Haverfordwest and Milford Haven Telegraph* dated 2nd January, 1856. The desirable and genteel residence was to let. The ground floor comprised dining room, drawing room and library, kitchen, pantry, scullery and dairy. On the first floor were five main bedrooms and two servants' rooms. Beneath the house were three cellars. Outbuildings included coach-houses and stables with two further bedrooms for servants. A walled garden in front of

13. Y Fagwr, formerly Rock House, first of the town houses owned by the Williams family.

the house gave rise to the original name, Fagwr gaiad, of the property.

The house was then some twenty years old. On 13th October, 1835, Rev. Jonah Owen, vicar choral and master of the Cathedral Grammar School, had purchased several fields near Lower Moor, including Fagwr gaiad, from John Hill Harries of Priskilly. Shortly afterwards the house and offices were built on the site. Jonah Owen had, on 4th June, 1833, married Mary Anne, elder daughter of George Williams of Old Shop; it was Mr. Williams who had provided much of the money needed for the erection of the house.

Jonah Owen had been appointed master in 1829, when the school was apparently located in the present Cathedral Library. The school catered not only for boys from the locality, but also for the sons of clergymen and the gentry of the county. Presumably it was the intention of Rev. Owen to use the commodious Rock House to house the school.

Sadly on 8th September, 1839, Rev. Owen died leaving a widow and three young daughters. After some delay Rev. Nathaniel Davies was appointed to take over the school. Later, in an acrimonious dispute with Dean Lewellin, he accused the church authorities of delay in appointing him to the post and of failure to provide accommodation for the school. For a time it continued at Rock House, where Rev. Davies was living with his wife and children at the time of the 1841 census. Also living there were sixteen boys whose ages ranged from eight to fifteen years; all were described as classical scholars. Meanwhile Mrs. Owen had taken up residence in the house adjoining the lowest granary.

The school did not remain for long at Rock House. During the following year it moved, its more permanent home being Grove House at the upper end of High Street. Samuel Williams (brother of Mary Anne Owen) married Elizabeth Owen of Hendre in November 1841. They made their home at Rock House, and were certainly in residence by the following September when their eldest son George Owen Williams was born.

The personal estate of Rev. Owen was small and proved insufficient to cover his commitments. The house had to be sold to cover his debts and to pay for various bequests in his will. Auctioned at the Commercial Inn on 6th August, 1844, it was purchased for £900 by Elizabeth Williams of Old Shop. Rock House remained in the family, but at a cost.

The spacious, airy apartments of Rock House contrasted sharply with the dark, low-ceilinged, oak-beamed rooms of Old Shop. It was a house to be lived in and enjoyed. Samuel Williams had the money to furnish it comfortably and fashionably; he was much more a man of the world than his father and he enjoyed his pleasures. He and his wife could afford to entertain their friends and relations and they could afford to dress well and expensively. The old folks who remembered those days told of how they would ride to chapel in their private coach; memories which were handed down through the generations. It was a time of prosperity.

Samuel Williams was a man of action. He had taken on the corn and culm merchant side of the family business as well as the lime burning at Porthclais. He expanded the shipping interests and became a Lloyd's Agent. He showed a keen interest in the education of the young and he played an important part in the life of the chapel. But it was not all hard work as far as he was concerned.

Like most country gentlemen he took pleasure in rural pastimes. He was a keen angler, he spent many happy hours boating, he enjoyed shooting and he kept dogs for coursing. And he loved writing about these pursuits. In an article in a local paper, written many years later, he described how he and a friend, while on a shooting expedition, had come across a hoopoe - even then an uncommon bird. They had stalked it for some time, but as soon as they came within range the bird would fly off. At last they succeeded in getting close enough to their prey. Samuel was on the point of firing when a falcon swooped down and carried off the hapless hoopoe. He was not afraid to tell a story against himself.

Already a successful man of business, Samuel was not yet twenty five when his second son William Watts was born in March 1844. But there was sadness as well as joy; a third son and a daughter died in infancy. At that time even in relatively prosperous families infant mortality was high; the tombstone of Samuel's uncle William Williams of Penlan and his wife carries the inscription: "Eleven of their children are buried near the same place" - the oldest of these was aged 9, though four others survived to a mature age.

In 1851 Samuel inherited Lower Treginnis from his kinsman Henry Harries. Samuel, always ready for a challenge, decided to move to the farm. His mother, almost seventy years of age, took up residence at Rock House. Three years later disaster struck when her eldest son Ebenezer, the druggist, was declared bankrupt. To help out, Mrs. Williams was forced to raise a mortgage of £1,500 on her property. In March 1855 she sold Rock House to Samuel who still lived at Treginnis. By now the house was becoming too large for her. So it was that in the following March a tenant was being sought for Rock House.

Later that year Samuel Williams moved to Cardiff; Rock House was sold. What was, and perhaps still is, the most desirable residence in St. David's passed out of the hands of the Williams family. It was a sale that in later years the family may well have had cause to regret.

VI; A Mysterious Legacy

To Henry and Anne Harries of Lower Treginnis the birth of a son, John Raymond, on 28th September, 1816, was a cause for great rejoicing. It meant continuity, so important to the farming community, and Henry Harries could trace his ancestors at the farm for over two centuries.

At the start of the seventeenth century, the tenant at Lower Treginnis had been Thomas Philip David; he was succeeded by his namesake-son, and Davids occupied the farm until the end of the century. Peter Lewis, subchanter of the cathedral, in his Journal, records a sad little episode concerning some of the last of the family to bear that name:

> "The wife of Harry David of Tregynis was buried on ye 17th of Aug: 1697: died in childbed, the child surviving."
> "Harry David of Tregynus was buried on ... of December 1697."
> "The son of Harry David of Tregynus, an Infant and an Orphan fell into scalding water and died in four days after and was buried ye 11th of October 1700."

About this time the family adopted the surname Harries, and John Raymond was the latest in that line. For much of the early part of the eighteenth century, the farm was occupied by Thomas Harries whose wife Eleanor was a daughter of John Harries of Cryglas. Thomas was made a lay vicar choral in 1702 but was suspended for drunkenness in 1725; he was later reinstated.

Thomas Harries died in 1727; he was succeeded at Lower Treginnis by his son-in-law Rev. James Roberts, vicar choral, who had married his daughter Anne. His son John Harries had married Anne Rees of Upper Treginnis and had become tenant of Ramsey Island. In 1763 James Roberts (junior) of Lower Treginnis married his first cousin Martha Harries. Following the death of James Roberts (senior) the tenancy was taken over for some time by Thomas Rees before passing to the younger James Roberts. In spite of the change in names they were all related to the original Harries family. In 1788 both Upper and Lower Treginnis were sold by their owners, the Owens of Great Nash in Llangwm parish, and James Roberts became owner-occupier of the former.

Lower Treginnis was purchased by Henry Harries (senior) who was farming on Ramsey Island. Henry, a son of John and Anne Harries, had married Elizabeth Williams of Upper Treginnis in 1767; their two children, Martha and Henry (junior), had been born on the island. The family returned to the mainland to Lower Treginnis where Henry (senior) died in 1798. The farm passed to his widow and afterwards to his only son. In 1813 Henry Harries (junior) married Anne Raymond at

14. The old farmhouse with its round chimney at Lower Treginnis as it was in 1806; the storehouse on the right survives almost unchanged.

Whitchurch. She was a member of the wealthy merchant family of Raymond of Solva and owned a number of properties in Whitchurch parish.

The joy which Henry and Anne Harries experienced at the birth of their son was to be short lived; John Raymond died when he was only 17 days old. They had no other children, the line of succession was broken. Martha Harries, sister of the younger Henry, had married Thomas Griffiths, master mariner of Solva; they also had no children. The nearest other relatives of Henry Harries were the Williams family of Old Shop.

There was a close connection between the two families, in which brother and sister from Lower Treginnis had married sister and brother from Upper Treginnis. On 29th December, 1767, Henry Harries (senior) had married Elizabeth Williams; almost a year later Anne Harries had married Henry Williams. The latter couple had farmed at Upper Treginnis until it had been destroyed by fire; they had then moved into St. David's and taken over the Old Shop.

The Harries family, like their cousins, became Nonconformists in the early nineteenth century. But Henry Harries (junior) and his wife were Wesleyan Methodists; Henry Harries was one of the original trustees of

Bethel Chapel which was erected in Goat Street in 1818. He also contributed handsomely to its later extension and left money to the chapel in his will.

According to Francis Green, Henry was an active (at times too active) member of the congregation. He was well known for making audible comments on the sermon: "Quite right, Jim! Quite right!" if he agreed. But, sometimes his remarks were far from complimentary to the preacher, and, on at least one occasion he had to be forcibly removed from the chapel.

His eccentricity was apparently not confined to his religion. He was the owner of a peculiar two-wheeled carriage, known locally as 'dwmbwr, dwmbwr', in which he would ride from Treginnis to the chapel. But, for all that, he was a successful farmer. Also, he saw the potential of the copper ores which lay under his land, and during the 1820s he leased the mining rights to the Stephens brothers, though this enterprise proved unsuccessful, And presumably it was Henry who first built the Georgian farmhouse which replaced the earlier round-chimneyed house on the site.

Henry and Anne grew old together, but it was Anne who died first, on 30th March, 1850. Had Henry died first the estate would have passed to his widow, and, after her days, at least the property which had originally belonged to her would presumably have reverted to the Raymonds. Henry's sister was already dead, so Treginnis itself would perhaps have passed to the Williamses.

But it was Henry who survived, and he had ideas of his own. On 30th May he drew up his will. The witnesses were no mere farm servants; they were men of standing: James Propert Williams, vicar of Whitchurch; Samuel Roberts, vicar choral; and Edward Loveling Bevan, surgeon, of St. David's. His executors were Samuel Williams, merchant, son of his first cousin, and William Richardson, perpetual curate of St. David's. Henry Harries was determined that the will's validity was beyond question.

Henry did not long outlive his wife; he died on 6th July. According to Francis Green, when the end was near Samuel Williams arrived at Treginnis with a keg of whisky. The two men had then spent the hours until Henry's death alternately praying and drinking. It would have caused comment among the ardent teetotallers of Bethel, but the contents of the will must have caused a sensation.

There were bequests to the chapel and its minister, and there were other minor bequests. Lower Treginnis was left to Samuel Williams. But the bulk of his property was left in trust "to ..... my dear friend Mary Anne Griffiths who now lives with me during her natural life." Afterwards it was to pass to any child born to her in wedlock. The property, originally that belonging to the Raymonds, was extensive. It included

Llaingamma in Whitchurch parish, and a considerable number of cottages at Llaingamma, in Upper Solva, and elsewhere in the parish. Mary Anne Griffiths was now a comparatively wealthy woman. Who was she?

In spite of her surname she was not a daughter of Thomas and Martha Griffiths. At the time of the 1851 census she was living at Fagwr gaiad with Elizabeth Williams - Samuel's mother. Aged 21 she is described as 'niece'; but that was an honorary title. On the occasion of her marriage she is recorded as having been born in Whitchurch parish, but where her father's name should appear is a blank.

There the trail goes cold; she cannot be identified with certainty in the previous census. What was her connection with Henry Harries, and why (only a couple of months after his wife's death) was she his "dear friend Mary Anne Griffiths"?

If Owie Williams knew, it was something he did not pass on to his young listeners in the Bank.

15. The modern farmhouse at Lower Treginnis which replaced the earlier thatched home of Henry Harries.

37

VII; Bristol Traders

There was living in St. David's in the year 1835, according to a Report of the Commissioners on Municipal Corporations in England and Wales, one man: "who keeps the only respectable shop in the City, and at whose expense the pier is kept in repair." That man was George Williams.

During the first quarter of the nineteenth century, George Williams had become involved in the purchase of shares in a number of small sailing vessels which traded to and from Porthclais. His partners, who held shares in one or more of these ships, were his brother John Williams of Clegyr, George Perkins and John Perkins, both of Porthllisky, and William Davies of Rhosson; all were farmers. And in each ship there was one other who held shares - the master of the vessel, men like John Rees of *Favourite Nancy*, Thomas Hughes of *Betsey* and Henry Grinnis of *Kitty*.

The earliest of the ships for which complete details of ownership are known (Milford Registers are incomplete before 1827) was the 23 ton smack *Favourite Nancy*, built at Milford in 1817. Two years later the slightly larger sloop *Betsey* of 28 tons, also newly built at Milford, was purchased. In 1829 the 25 ton Lawrenny-built sloop *Kitty* joined the fleet. Almost certainly there were others; *Mary* of 19 tons, perhaps built in 1825, and *Eliza* which may have been at one time tender to the Smalls lighthouse.

Favourite Nancy was not the first boat owned by George Williams. During the year previous to her construction, Mr. Williams had sent one of his ships to Liverpool to obtain timber for the new chapel which was then being erected in Goat Street. It proved (according to D. Idwal Jones) to be a long and stormy voyage. Only after many perilous adventures did the unnamed vessel reach the safety of Porthclais, with her crew - including John Williams of Clegyr - and cargo intact.

Why did George Williams become so deeply involved with shipping? In the early nineteenth century most of the manufactured and shop goods were carried to the towns and villages of West Wales, chiefly from Bristol, in small coastal sloops. It was to George's advantage to have an interest in the ships which brought these goods. Much of the trade of Old Shop was with the farming community, and involved bartering the shop goods for agricultural produce. Some of this was sold in the shop, but the surplus grain, butter and cheese were exported in the sloops to Bristol. George Williams had also become a lime burner and when the ships were not engaged on the Bristol run they spent their time carrying culm and limestone to Porthclais to feed the ever rapacious appetites of the kilns.

According to the 1835 Report George Williams was responsible for the entire export trade from Porthclais which consisted of corn (chiefly

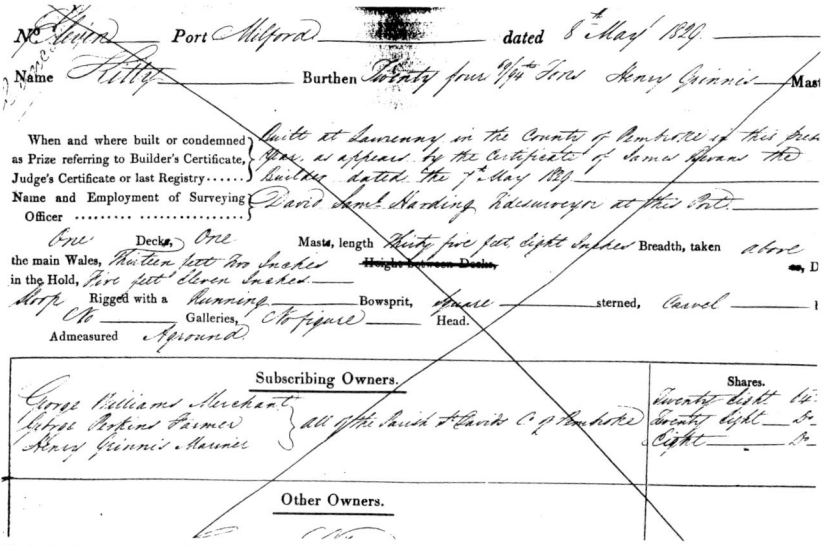

Original entry on Register of Kitty *at Port of Milford, 8th May, 1829.*

barley) and butter. Pigot's *Directory* of 1830 names the ships: *Kitty*, master Henry Grinnis; *Mary*, George James; *Favourite Nancy*, John Rees. Samuel Lewis, writing in 1833, mentions that the harbour and pier had recently been improved, and that the exports to Bristol took place mainly during the winter. Otherwise, trade was largely confined to importing culm and limestone.

In all this George Williams was deeply involved. He operated the limekilns at Porthclais. He purchased the two lower granaries on the road to Porthclais; in these he could store the corn which he had purchased until the winter months when it would fetch the highest price. It was his ships in which the corn was carried, and in which limestone from the shores of Milford Haven and culm from Nolton and Hook were brought to Porthclais.

As far as George Williams was concerned, his maritime activities were a sideline to his major interests as merchant and shopkeeper. His involvement was almost entirely confined to coastal sloops in which he owned between 16 and 32 of the 64 shares into which by law each was divided. His sole known essay into larger vessels was his purchase of 4 shares in the 106 ton schooner *Mary Ellen* which was registered at Newport (Gwent) in 1833. But his son Samuel who eventually succeeded to the merchant and shipping side of the business was in many respects a very different person.

16. The smack Albatross *at Llangrannog c. 1900; the last survivor of the ships once owned by Samuel Williams, and the only one of which a photograph is known to exist.*

While his father had spent his early years on the farm, Samuel Williams had been involved with the sea from an early age. As a young boy he would have accompanied his father to Porthclais to meet the incoming ships. He would have known their captains like John Rees of Rhosson, and perhaps would have sailed with him on *Favourite Nancy* across the bay to Nolton to fetch culm to burn in the kilns. Like his father, Samuel obtained his early education at the Cathedral Grammar School; later he attended the Prospect Place Academy in Bristol, where the headmaster was George Pocock. To reach Bristol he sailed in one or other of the family boats, no doubt acting as an honorary member of the crew for the duration of the voyage. Later still, according to his father's will, he was: "fitted for the sea-service at a cost of about fifty pounds." And, in a letter to an old shipmate, written many years later, he refers to the happy times spent aboard the old *Wellington*.

At the time of his father's death in 1838, Samuel was a mere lad of nineteen. At first his mother carried on the family business, including the shipping. However, within a year, he and his older brother Ebenezer had each purchased 16 shares (later increased to 20) in the newly built smack *Rechabite* of 19 tons register. By this time of the old family boats only *Favourite Nancy* and *Kitty* survived. No doubt at Samuel's suggestion the shares held by the family in the former were disposed of in May 1842; barely two years later *Favourite Nancy* was declared unseaworthy. The shares in *Kitty* were retained and Samuel eventually acquired all 64 shares. *Kitty* continued to sail the seas for another three decades. Samuel, even at an early age, undoubtedly had an eye for business.

Over the succeeding years Samuel Williams became the owner of a number of other vessels. First of these was the 20 ton *True Bess*, newly built at Aberayron in 1846. In 1847 he purchased the 28 ton, Milford-built, *Albatross*, though she was sold a year later. Also in 1847 he bought a much larger vessel - the 132 ton brigantine *Talent*. Unlike his other ships, which were mere coasters, *Talent* was used in the timber trade with North America; by this time Samuel had established himself as a timber merchant as well as coal and corn merchant and lime burner. Sometime during the next few years he purchased two more sloops; the *Valiant* (originally owned by the Grinnis family of Porthmawr and registered in 1835 at 18 tons) and the slightly smaller *Sisters*. With the exception of *Rechabite*, he was the sole owner; by 1850 he was by far the most important shipowner based at Porthclais.

The maritime activities of Samuel Williams were not confined to owning and operating ships. On 11th December, 1850, he was appointed as official Lloyd's Agent for St. David's. He was the first person to hold that office; though he had apparently served as sub-agent since 1839, when St. David's was a sub-agency under Milford. He was not the first member of the family to hold the latter position. According to an entry in the Williams Letter Books his father, George Williams, had been sub-agent for some twenty years up to the time of his death in 1838.

The area covered by the St. David's Agency included the coast from Penclegyr (near Porthgain) to Newgale Bridge, together with Ramsey and the adjacent islands. The post of Agent for Lloyd's was a responsible one,

---

ST. DAVID'S.

QUEBEC TIMBER FOR SALE.

NOW on SALE, at ST. DAVID'S, a very choice CARGO of QUEBEC TIMBER, just Imported ex Brigantine "Talent," by SAMUEL WILLIAMS, consisting of Oak, Ash, Elm, Red and Yellow Pine, Deals, Deal Ends, Oak and Ash Staves, &c. &c.

St. David's, Dec. 5, 1854.

Haverfordwest & Milford Haven Telegraph, Wednesday, 6th December, 1854.

and to achieve it required the support of a number of eminent men connected with maritime affairs. Barely thirty years of age, Samuel Williams had already established himself as a widely known and trusted man of business.

As a Lloyd's Agent he was required to note the ships which called and those which passed, and, when necessary, to report to headquarters. The trade of the harbours at Solva and Porthclais was almost exclusively coastal, so that this task was hardly onerous. But, along this hazardous and unpredictable coast, his most important function was in dealing with the vessels which became wrecked; for assessing the extent of the loss, and where possible arranging for the salvage of vessel and cargo. There was much to do! But to Samuel it was a task he relished. Active in mind and body, the investigation of the circumstances of the loss and the subsequent writing of the report provided an outlet for his energy. Over a period of a little over forty years from about 1825 there were, by his own account, more than seventy wrecks involving insurance in the area, many of them during his tenure of the office.

His new-found status as Lloyd's Agent in no way affected Samuel Williams' own activities. During the 1850s (according to Slater's *Directory*) his sloops *Kitty* and *Rechabite*, together with *William* (whose owner and master was Thomas Hughes of Porthclais) sailed monthly to Bristol. The Agent for the Bristol Traders was Samuel Williams. Nothing had really changed in over a quarter of a century, and it must have seemed that nothing ever would.

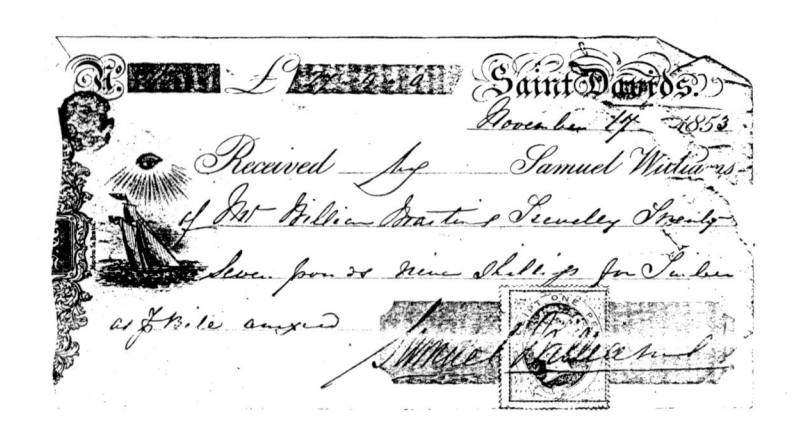

VIII; A Financial Disaster

On the morning of Thursday, 24th August, 1854, the normally placid streets and alleys of St. David's were alive with people gathered conspiratorially together in small groups. What had started as a whispered rumour: "Have you heard?" soon became the openly expressed statement: "Ebenezer Williams has gone bankrupt."

Some said: "Poor Mrs. Williams!" Others nodded wisely when they heard, implying that they had known all along that something was amiss. One or two could scarcely conceal their satisfaction.

It seemed incredible; Ebenezer Williams, the druggist, a bankrupt! Ebenezer, eldest son of Elizabeth Williams of Rock House and of the late George Williams, Old Shop; surely it couldn't be true! Not Ebenezer, pillar of Methodism at Tabernacle and active worker in the field of education! After all he was the man with whom many of them had taken out insurance. Could anyone be trusted?

It was true enough. Ebenezer had overstretched his resources. To cover the debts which he had incurred he had been forced to borrow. The profits from his shop, his farm and his rents were not sufficient to sustain his mode of living and, at the same time, to pay his creditors. The inevitable happened; his debts were called in, and, when he could not meet them, bankruptcy was the only course open to him.

Only some six years previously Ebenezer had built the imposing Georgian house on Cross Square - the present Menai. He had furnished it lavishly and lived there with his wife and two children in a style to match. There, in a part of the building designed as a shop, he had set up his business as druggist and grocer.

In addition he farmed at Trecenny; he owned several fields near Lower Mill and three cottages at Mount Gardens in New Street. He had a small interest in shipping; apart from his shares in *Rechabite* he had inherited 8 shares in the 106 ton schooner *Mary Ellen* and 4 in the 113 ton brig *Victory*, both registered at Milford. He also owned shares in, and was local representative for, the Farmers General Life and Fire Insurance Company

The rumour was that Mr. Williams owed the not inconsiderable sum of about £11,000 in total. How had this come about? He certainly lived well, and perhaps had made some unwise speculations; but these hardly explained the extent of his debts. What then was the cause of his failure?

The problem had begun many years earlier. George Williams, the merchant, had prospered greatly. Some of his profits went into improving and expanding his business and into buying ships. Some he invested in property, in land and in warehouses. And some he lent as mortgage on the property of others.

17. Menai on Cross Square; the shop window betrays its origin as the home of the druggist Ebenezer Williams.

In November 1832 he had loaned a sum of £1,800 as mortgage on Upper Treginnis - his birthplace - to John Roberts and his daughter Emily, the widow of John Mortimer. The farm had been originally purchased by James Roberts (father of John) in 1788, a few years after the fire which had destroyed the livelihood of Henry Williams. Emily, "who (according to the Parish Register) was scalded to death by falling into a tub of boiling wort", and her father had since died, and the property had passed to her eldest son John Mortimer. Then, in November 1838 George Williams had also died.

Repayments on the loan had been made up to the time of George's death, but had then ceased; John Mortimer refusing to make further payments. Elizabeth Williams (widow and executrix of George Williams) had taken legal advice, and a Draft Bill in Chancery had been prepared. The original case had been heard at the Summer Assizes for 1842 at Haverfordwest. The verdict was in favour of the plaintiff, but this was later set aside.

It was a scenario worthy of Dickens. There were disputes as to relationships and successions. There were witnesses who could not be found and others who had since died. There were arguments concerning the precise terms of wills, of entails and of earlier mortgages. The dispute

> ST. DAVID'S, PEMBROKESHIRE.
>
> To Druggists, Grocers, Oil and Colourmen, and Fancy Stationers.
>
> MESSRS. BARNARD, THOMAS, and Co. have received instructions to dispose of by PRIVATE CONTRACT, the very excellent STOCK and BUSINESS of Mr. EBENEZER WILLIAMS, of St. David's, who is retiring therefrom. The Business—which is the only one of the kind in the place—has been carried on for about Six Years, with a good connection. Stock about £500, and may be taken immediately.
>
> For all further particulars, apply to the BROKERS, Albion Chambers, Bristol; or to their ASSISTANT, on the Premises, at St. David's.

Haverfordwest & Milford Haven Telegraph, Wednesday, 6th September, 1854.

dragged on for years. In the end Mrs. Williams lost not only the original £1,800 and the large amount of interest due, but also the considerable charges of the legal advisers.

It was money that George Williams had worked hard to earn, and it was money the family could ill-afford to lose. But Ebenezer Williams continued to pursue the matter long after the case was irretrievably lost. The legal costs continued to mount. For Ebenezer it was the beginning of the slippery slope to disaster.

The Petition for Bankruptcy against Ebenezer Williams; druggist, grocer, farmer, dealer and chapman, was filed at the Bristol Court of Bankruptcy on 5th September, 1854. The hearings were set for 26th September and 24th October when he was to appear in person.

Already a notice had appeared in the local press in early September, concerning the sale of the contents of the shop. That was only the beginning. On Tuesday, 10th October, the sale was to take place, on the orders of the Court of Bankruptcy, of the crops and implements at Trecenny belonging to Ebenezer Williams, bankrupt. There was no reserve; there were bargains to be had by the purchasers.

On the following day the household effects at Cross Square were for sale. They included: mahogany wardrobes, tables, chairs, sideboards and chiffoniers; fourposter, tent and French bedsteads; Kidderminster and Brussels carpets and rugs - his entire home. Later the same day Ebenezer's shipping and other shares were for disposal. It must have been a traumatic experience for Ebenezer and Martha Williams. Everything they had worked for was to go.

The rest of the family rallied round. His brother Samuel raised a considerable mortgage on his shipping and other assets. His mother arranged an auction of much of her property: three houses, two warehouses and a smithy in Catherine Street; ten fields near Lower Moor, six at the Morfa (west of St. Non's Bay) and two at Tir-y-bar (near the Burrows); in all thirteen lots - to take place on 18th October. In the event, most of this was not actually sold.

On 10th January, 1855, Ebenezer appeared once more at the Court of Bankruptcy. The official report stated that many of the debts had been contracted to pay off old liabilities. No cash book had been kept, but otherwise the report was favourable and Mr. Williams was awarded his Certificate of Bankruptcy.

Even that was not the end! The *Haverfordwest and Milford Haven Telegraph* of 7th February contained an announcement of the sale, to take place on 5th March at the Commercial Inn, of the house on Cross Square, three cottages and land in New Street, and fields near Lower Mill.

The shame proved too much. A mere eighteen months later Ebenezer Williams died a broken man. He was only 44 years of age.

IX; A Liverpool Interlude

A notice in the *Haverfordwest and Milford Haven Telegraph* of 2nd January, 1856, informed its readers that Samuel Williams of Lower Treginnis was giving up his business as a merchant. His four remaining sloops were for sale and his two corn stores - the only ones in St. David's - were to be let, as was Rock House. On 20th June the same paper announced that Lower Treginnis was itself to be sold by auction.

Samuel Williams, like his father before him, was leaving St. David's. But, unlike his father, Samuel was by then in his late thirties and had already built up a large and successful business. Obviously the failure of his brother's business had affected him, but there were other clouds on the horizon. Most significant among these was the arrival of the railway some two years previously at Haverfordwest, threatening the future of the coastal trade on which the fortunes of the Williams family (and many others) had depended in the first half of the century. Future prosperity, as he saw it, lay elsewhere.

He moved with his wife and three young sons to Cardiff and, within the year, to Liverpool. His chosen profession in this rapidly developing port was that of ship-broker; this involved chartering ships to carry cargo, and arranging the best possible terms for the owner of the cargo. As a merchant and shipowner, and as the Lloyd's Agent for St. David's, Samuel Williams was already well known to many of the owners and masters of ships trading with Liverpool.

In order to familiarise himself with the ship-broking business, Samuel took up a position with the firm of Cole and Jones who had offices at 18, Brunswick Street, in the commercial part of the city. Soon he had achieved a position of responsibility with the company. It was no sinecure: the hours were long and the work demanding. Some mornings would find him down at the Pier Head by half past seven and he might not return home until after eight in the evening, having visited many ships in the meantime. But to the ever ambitious Samuel it was experience for the time when he would establish his own firm of ship-brokers.

Home to the family at one time was in Roscommon Street, Everton - a street of early nineteenth century houses, most of which were occupied by respectable middle-class families. The house was commodious and comfortable, with a garden where they could grow their own produce. But, to a family used to the expanses of Treginnis and Rock House it must have seemed strange and confining to live in a built-up street in a large city. Gone were the opportunities for riding and shooting and fishing which they had enjoyed back in Pembrokeshire; instead, for the younger members of the family there was cricket.

There were compensations. There was a large and energetic Welsh community in Liverpool; merchants, shipowners and sea captains among them. Some came from Pembrokeshire, and there were flourishing Welsh societies, in particular the chapels. At that time there were probably more Welsh-speakers in Liverpool than in any town in Wales. Before long the Williamses were part of this close-knit community and, being relatively affluent, with servants to run the home, they could entertain, and be entertained by, their friends as much as ever.

On 24th April, 1862, Samuel Williams made his long intended move. On that day he set up as ship-broker "on my own hoof" (as he expressed it) at 17, Back Goree, Brunswick Street. He was exchanging a secure position with one of the leading firms in the port for a dingy office in a back street. He had behind him four years as chartering clerk with Messrs. Cole and Jones; in that time he had familiarised himself with the trade of the port, and with the men and ships involved in it. It was a bold move and it entailed risks. From now on success lay entirely in his own hands.

His first task, as evidenced by his surviving letter book, was to advertise his new status. Letters to ship-brokers and shipowners in Cardiff, London, Glasgow, Newcastle and elsewhere; letters to masters, many of them old friends; letters to merchants in West Wales, in Cardigan, Fishguard and Aberystwyth; letters by the dozen were despatched around the country in the following days. But, in all this activity, the very first letter was to Mrs. Jenkins of Llandigige Fach to inform her that her husband's ship had berthed at Liverpool. There was still time for the common touch.

There were cargoes available: 200 tons of guano from Liverpool to Ghent; 150 tons of pig iron to Dunkirk; 150 tons of flour in sacks from Portrieux, near St. Malo; 150 tons of oil from Scala Nova; 170 tons of rough salt from Figuera; and above all coal. But there was fierce competition with other brokers and between the masters of various ships. It was hard work, and there was no guarantee of gaining the charter.

Liverpool had been badly affected by the American blockade - it was the time of the American Civil War. The American trade was, as Samuel Williams wrote in one of his letters: "the life and soul of our business and the want of it makes all things very dull." Trade was not improved by the inclement weather of the summer; in late July the river and docks were full of outward bound vessels, some of which had been waiting to sail for over three weeks.

It was hard work and the hours were long - perhaps longer than when he had worked for Messrs. Cole and Jones. There were visits to the docks to talk with captains of ships, and to the Angel Hotel to meet company representatives. The person he sought could not always be found and then there were more letters to be sent to make new appointments.

At first, charters were hard to come by; it took time to make the right contacts. His friend, George Gould of Milford, was able to supply him with the names of recently established shipowners in Pembrokeshire to add to those he already knew. Gradually conditions improved and commissions began to appear. He was aware that he lacked capital, but the day arrived when he snatched a contract from under the noses of his former employers. On 2nd August he was able to write to Captain Humphreys of the *Agenoria* at Haverfordwest that the previous week had been very profitable. On that very day he had earned £86 for chartering the *Orinoco* for Brest.

Although well established in the hurried life of the great seaport, there was still a feeling of 'hiraeth' for his native Wales. On 25th July he wrote to his old friend and one-time rival as merchant and shipowner John Williams of the Ship Hotel in Solva:

"I should be very glad to have 'Quiet Pipe' with you on the old settle and although I am a strict Teetotaller in practice would be tempted to have a 'swig' of your good beer, and would be sure to have a chance at your rod and line from the bridge down. I have not 'Thrown a fly' these five years, but fancy I have not forgotten how to do so altogether."

In the event Samuel was to have his opportunity much sooner than he anticipated. On 7th August he wrote letter number 217; it was to be the last entry in the book. His career as a Liverpool ship-broker had come to an abrupt end.

X; The Watts Harris Inheritance

On 6th August, 1862, there died at Goat Street, Haverfordwest, aged 63, Rev. William Watts Harris, Rector of Prendergast, Chaplain to Haverfordwest Gaol and Prebendary of Caerfai. A widower and childless, the principal beneficiary of his considerable estate was his only niece Elizabeth.

Prebendary Watts Harris was descended on his father's side from the Hendre family and on his mother's side from the Watts family of Hayscastle. The latter family had been associated with the parish of Hayscastle at least since the seventeenth century; in 1670, Jane Watts (widow of John Watts of Brimaston) was assessed at four hearths. Over half a century later, John Watts of Hayscastle, apparently a great-nephew of his Brimaston namesake, married Phebe Williams of St. David's, a member of the Caerforiog family.

The young couple took up residence at Hayscastle, in the old farmhouse which stood opposite the tiny church of the same name. There they prospered greatly. By the time of his death in 1755, John Watts owned not only the large farm of Hayscastle itself, but also the farm of Brynyscawen in Brawdy parish, land in Llanhowell parish and property in and around the town of St. David's. They became prominent Methodists and entertained many of the visiting preachers on their travels between Haverfordwest and St. David's; most notable among these was the great revivalist Howel Harris.

Subject to a life interest in Hayscastle to his widow, John Watts willed the bulk of his estate to his only son William. He also left £400 to his only daughter Damaris when she reached the age of sixteen. Surprisingly, in an age when little value was placed on the education of girls, a sum of £8 per annum was put towards this purpose until that time. Appointed as guardians were: Mr. Evan Thomas of Llanbadarn Venydd, Radnor; Mrs. Elizabeth Rowlands and Miss Hannah Bowen, both of Llanidloes, and Mr. Howel Harris of Talgarth. Obviously the Watts family were people of some significance.

William Watts and his wife Dorothy (Phelps of Cresselly) had six children. Their three sons - Henry, Peter and John - remained bachelors, while their daughter Dorothy also died unmarried. Of the others, Lettice, who married a Mr. Rees of Haverfordwest, had three daughters, and only Phebe, who married William Harris of Hendre and had two clergymen sons, produced a male heir.

After the death of her husband in 1782, Dorothy Watts (the elder), who survived him by thirty six years, continued to live at Hayscastle with her unmarried children. The property passed first to Henry, the eldest son, and on his death in 1794 to the second son Peter. The rambling old house at Hayscastle must have been a strange home, with the old mother, three bachelor brothers and spinster sister living together. Strange too, that, in a period when land and succession to the land was so important, none of the brothers should marry.

Gone were the days when Hayscastle echoed to the hymns and prayers of the visiting preachers and their enthusiastic followers. The isolated old farmhouse, seven miles north of Haverfordwest, remote from any village, grew ever more lonely as its inhabitants grew older. Little disturbed the peace other than the clamour of the rooks in the trees around the church. One by one the family died; first Henry, then his mother Dorothy in 1818. For another quarter of a century her three children lived together in the house which grew old with them. John died in 1843, his sister Dorothy a year later, and only Peter - nearly eighty years old - was left.

The simple life they led meant that the family became progressively more wealthy. In his later years, when farming was prosperous, and particularly so for the more fertile farms like Hayscastle, Peter Watts was able to add considerably to his estates. He purchased Carregwen in Letterston parish, Vagwreilw in Llanhowell and several properties in St. Lawrence, including Creigiau, Llainygored, Banal, Butts, Llainddu, Trerhos, Penparc and Plaindealings. When he died on 21st May, 1847, aged 82, he was able to settle £500 on each of his five nieces, including Jane Rees who lived with him. The bulk of his estate was bequeathed to his only surviving nephew, Rev. William Watts Harris of Haverfordwest, formerly of Hendre in St. David's parish.

By this time the Harris family of Hendre were also relatively affluent, though this had not always been the case. As Samuel Williams wrote in his 'Family Chronology':

"Evan Harry of St David's was the father of William Harry or Harries (afterwards) of Hendre - but I have no further record excepting Wm. Harries (my grandfather in law) that he was born at Trefecca (a then farm) part of Hendre eynon. The farm house was situated in the hollow of the first of the Hendre eynon fields on the left hand going north. Mr. Harries was addopted by an uncle residing at Hendre and who left him all his property. Mr. Harries by an Indenture in my possession dated 8 March 1779 bound himself apprentice to Henry Phillips (Emlych) covn two pounds per annum - to learn the trade of farming. I am inclined to think that this was for the purpose of being free from Compulsory Military Service."

Two miles outside St. David's, just north of the main road to Fishguard, stands the imposing mid-nineteenth century farmhouse of Hendre. Its level acres of fertile land stretch from the southern edge of Dowrog

19. The nineteenth century farmhouse at Hendre, once home to William Watts Williams.

Common southwards to the northern edge of St. David's Airfield. Even in the early nineteenth century many of the Hendre fields were large, but they were mostly divided haphazardly into 'slangs' and 'llains' belonging to a variety of owners. Some of these were owned by William Harris, others (including the old farmhouse where Mr. Harris lived) by Dr. Jones' Charity, still others by Thomas Rosser, a few by yet other owners. This patchwork of ownership, common in the area, must have made efficient farming almost impossible; often it led to angry disputes as to the boundaries and ownership of land. As it happened, William Harris became tenant of the remainder of the property, and was able to farm the land successfully. But it was many years before his descendants became the owners of all the land.

William, born in 1760, the son of Evan Harry and his wife Hester (nee Phillip) married Phebe Watts circa 1790 - probably at Hayscastle. By the marriage the families of Harris of Hendre and Watts of Hayscastle were linked. It was a socially advantageous marriage for William, as the Watts family were already prosperous, but he can have had no concept of how financially beneficial it would prove. After all Phebe had three brothers, any one of whom would inherit the estate before her; afterwards it would pass to his eldest son. Nevertheless, it was one of the children of William and Phebe - Elizabeth (born 1792), Hester (1794), John (1796) and

William Watts (1799) - who would in time inherit the estate. In the event the one who was "born with a silver spoon in his mouth" was the youngest, William Watts Harris.

Hester, the elder daughter, remained a spinster. In those days it was usual for the unmarried daughter of a farmer to remain at home to help on the farm. But Hester was more independent. She moved into St. David's and set up home in the rambling old house on the square which came to be known in later years as Old Cross. Here as a woman of independent means she was able to live in a state of some comfort.

On 2nd August, 1817, Elizabeth the younger daughter married John Owen the only son of Thomas Owen, master mariner, of Solva and his wife Elizabeth. John Owen was master of the 113 ton snow *Milford* in which he owned 28 shares. With the 5 shares held by his mother this was just sufficient to provide a controlling interest in the ship; 15 of the remaining shares were owned by his father-in-law. A comparatively large vessel, *Milford* did not trade locally, but was employed in the profitable pig trade from Southern Ireland. The young couple made their home at Hendre, where their only daughter Elizabeth was born on 13th November, 1819 - she was to become the wife of Samuel Williams.

John, the elder son of William and Phebe Harris, was, as a boy, a chorister in the cathedral. In 1820 he was appointed vicar choral at St. David's and vicar of St. Edrens; he resigned from the latter in 1832. In 1826 he became subchanter of St. David's and vicar of Llanwnda; the following year he was made perpetual curate of Uzmaston, and in 1832 vicar of Whitchurch; all these he held until his death in 1840. With scattered livings near Haverfordwest, Fishguard and St. David's it is hardly surprising that he was one of the subjects of an inquiry into the plurality of benefits. He remained a bachelor; after his death the estate he had acquired (subject to monetary bequests to close relatives) passed to his father. This property included Clegyrfwyaf and Trefaiddan.

The youngest of the family was William Watts Harris who, like his brother, entered the church. In 1824 he was appointed rector of Prendergast, and in 1835 Prebendary of Caerfai in St. David's Cathedral. At one time he lived in High Street, Haverfordwest, later he moved to a large house at the top of Goat Street. According to Canon Fuller he was guilty of neglecting both church and parish. On Sundays he would ride to church on his pony, seldom visiting otherwise except for weddings and funerals. He did nothing to restore the crumbling fabric of the church, and, when it rained, he would preach his sermon from under the protection of a raised umbrella.

On 27th October, 1831, Rev. Watts Harris married Dorothy Davies of Slade Cottage in the Hamlet of St. Martin; the wedding took place at St. Thomas Church, Haverfordwest. She was the widow of George Davies,

18. The house in Goat Street, Haverfordwest, which was the home of Prebendary William Watts Harris.

chemist and druggist, of Bridge Street, and daughter of Thomas Scowcroft, mercer, wine and timber merchant, of High Street, both in Haverfordwest. Thomas Scowcroft died in 1820 and the mercery and wine merchant business was inherited by his son William. The latter was declared bankrupt in March 1826; at the ensuing auction his estate was purchased by Rev. William Watts Harris.

William Harris of Hendre died on 8th December, 1842. During his lifetime he had acquired a number of properties mostly in and around St. David's. His estates were left to his wife for the duration of her life. After her death, which occurred a year later, Clegyrfwyaf and Trefaiddan, as well as land held by George Williams to the south of St. David's, were to pass to his son William Watts Harris. The remainder of his property in Cylch y dre, which included Pantybryn, Llain Caerfai, Llain Pendre and Tyllwyd, was assigned jointly to his daughters Hester Harris and Elizabeth Owen.

Rev. Watts Harris already owned a sizeable estate. Five years later on the death of his uncle Peter Watts of Hayscastle, this was increased still further. The rent book of Rev. Watts Harris around this time reveals the extent of his holdings. In 1853 no fewer than thirty three properties large and small are listed. The total rental for the half year ending on Lady Day was over £425.

In Brawdy the rent for Brynyscawen was over £21; in Eglwyswrw that for Carnhyan £35 and in Letterston for Carregwen £7. In the Chapelry of Mounton (near Narberth) the holding known as Mountain was worth £25, while two holdings in the Hamlet of St. Martin, Haverfordwest (one is still known as 'Harries Slade') came to £59, and in Llanhowell, two farms, Tresewig and Vagwreilw totalled £21. A rent charge on Parselle in St. Edren's accounted for £8, while Hayscastle itself at £85 was easily the most valuable.

But the majority of the properties were to be found in the parish of St. Lawrence and in St. David's itself. In the former, Upper and Lower Trerhos were together worth £59; ten other properties were altogether valued at about £54. In St. David's there were nine properties ranging from a barn in High Street let to widow Oakley for 1s.3d. to his one-third share of Hendre valued at £12. The total value for the parish was about £49; Trefeiddan and Clegyrfwyaf were together assessed at £17.

There were other acquisitions. When Ebenezer Williams was declared bankrupt, Rev. Watts Harris purchased property including the house on the square. As far as the Williams family was concerned it was a satisfactory outcome to the disaster.

Dorothy Watts Harris died on 13th December, 1855, at Haverfordwest. She left no children; Elizabeth, wife to Samuel Williams and niece to Rev. Watts Harris, was confirmed as his sole heiress, and it was a large estate to which she was entitled. Her uncle had inherited most of the Hendre estate from his father; the remainder had accrued to her mother and her aunt and that would eventually be hers. Rev. Watts Harris had, as the only male in his generation, inherited the bulk of the Hayscastle estate from his uncle Peter Watts; and there was property from his late wife Dorothy. And Elizabeth was the only member of her generation in her father's family; the Owens were not wealthy, but they did own some property in Solva. This too would come to her.

Samuel Williams was by no means poor, but by comparison with his wife his resources were limited. It was an old family saying: "Never marry for money, but marry where money is." Several of the family did make financially advantageous marriages, but by marrying his 'True Bess' Samuel made the most advantageous marriage of all.

As a woman, Elizabeth Williams would not inherit the Watts Harris estate in her own right; she and her husband would hold it in trust for her sons. Her eldest son George Owen Williams would eventually succeed to the property in Hayscastle and St. Lawrence; her second son William Watts Williams to the estate in St. David's and elsewhere. In the meantime Samuel and Elizabeth Williams would be able to live in comfort on their rents and interest. The youngest son John Harries Inkerman Williams, who was not born when Rev. Watts Harris drew up his will, eventually inherited most of the family possessions which did not form part of the Watts Harris estate.

So it was, when the news of the death of Rev. Watts Harris reached Liverpool, that Samuel Williams came home to St. David's. There was no longer any need for him to seek his own fortune as a ship-broker; in any case he was needed to take on the running of the estate. The abrupt end to the entries in the letter book of Samuel Williams, ship-broker, of 17, Back Goree, Liverpool, is explained.

Samuel was never to discover whether he could succeed on his "own hoof", but the likelihood is that given the opportunity he would have become a well-known figure around the docksides at Liverpool.

XI; The Commercial and the Grove

Of the four sons of Henry and Anne Williams of Treginnis and Old Shop, two - William and John - became farmers, while George took over the family business. Thomas, the second son, was originally trained as carpenter and cabinet maker.

It must have met with approval when Thomas married Martha Phillips in 1809. She came from a well-respected family; her father Henry Phillips was, and had been for many years, the Parish Clerk. The two families were already linked; some four years earlier Henry Phillips (junior) of Emlych had married Phebe Williams the only daughter of the Old Shop family.

Henry Phillips (junior) died young, leaving his widow with three daughters (including twins) and a son to bring up. John, the son, spent much of his boyhood at the Old Shop with his grandfather before learning the joinery trade with his uncle Thomas Williams.

When in 1825 his grandfather Henry Phillips began to fail in health, young John Phillips became his assistant. Two years later, on the death of the old clerk, John Phillips succeeded him. He lived on Cross Square, but most of the time the black-cloaked figure was to be found in and around the cathedral, where he acted as chief guide and verger. He became a leading authority on the cathedral building and its history, as well as on Welsh poetry and local folklore. For well over half a century he was clerk, and when he died in 1895, he and his grandfather had held the office for an incredible 118 years between them. Nobody was appointed to follow him; he was in any case irreplaceable.

The later career of Thomas Williams was more controversial. By 1828 he and his wife were to be found at the Commercial Inn, which stood in High Street opposite City Hall Lane. His new trade of innkeeper must have caused consternation in the two families; one Anglican, one Methodist, they would at least have been united in condemnation of the demon drink. The inn was however respectable enough to have been the meeting place for the Court of the Manor of City and Suburbs; in 1835 it was, according to Pigot, the only inn as opposed to tavern in the city.

Thomas Williams died in 1835. His widow carried on at the Commercial which she purchased from the Priskilly Estate in the same year. In 1841 she still lived there with two of her children - 25 year old Jane and 15 year old William. Ten years later, after his mother's death, William became landlord.

The new innkeeper was a man of ambition; he did not intend to spend his whole life as the mere keeper of a tavern. As it happened there were opportunities which would soon reveal themselves. In 1847 his sister Elizabeth had married John Rees, master mariner, the son of John Rees of Rhosson, the one-time master of the *Favourite Nancy*. John Rees (junior), then living in Liverpool, had purchased the 157 ton brigantine *Beaton* in 1851. In the following year William Williams had taken a half share in the *Beaton*, presumably to discharge a mortgage that Captain Rees had raised on the vessel. They operated the ship for a number of years, the first of several collaborations between them.

In 1856 Samuel Williams retired from business, prior to moving to Cardiff. It was the chance for which William was waiting! The two men were first cousins: both were successful merchants. But there were differences! Samuel was intelligent and extremely well-read, while William had limited education. Both were Methodists; Samuel was a well-respected deacon, while William was on at least one occasion suspended from membership.

But William was a man of character and certainly no fool. He took over much of the merchant trade which his cousin had operated. He became the chief lime burner in Porthclais, and he imported the artificial manure which largely replaced the lime trade. He was a coal and culm merchant as well as dealing in corn and butter. He purchased two of the

20. *The lowest of the granaries on the road to Porthclais. Once owned, with the two adjacent houses, by George Williams, Old Shop, it was later owned by William Williams, the Grove. All three granaries at one time belonged to the Williams family.*

granaries and exported the occasional cargo of corn from Porthclais until well into the 1890s. At a time when the coastal trade was on the wane he managed to operate profitably.

He became a shipowner in his own right. Over the succeeding years he acquired a number of small coastal vessels; most were sloops, but the *Maria and Fanny* was a schooner of 78 tons; purchased in July 1868 she was lost the following month. First of these coasters was the *Two Brothers*, a 22 ton smack, purchased in December 1858 and lost west of Ramsey in March 1872. Others lost in his ownership were *Courier*, wrecked at Porthclais in October 1879, and *Martha Jane* which came to grief on the Bitches in March 1894. Some, like *Otter*, were bought and later sold, but *Edith Williams* (named after one of his daughters) remained in his ownership at the time of his death in 1899. Sold five years later, she was perhaps the last of the coasters to be owned by one of the long-established St. David's families.

In 1869 William Williams left the Commercial to open the much larger and better Grove Hotel at the top of High Street. It had been built as a private house early in the nineteenth century, reputedly with stone from the ruinous Vicars' College in the Close. In 1840 it was owned and

21. Two coastal sloops moored at Porthclais c.1890; the nearer vessel can be identified as the Edith Williams; *Gilbert Martin, City Hotel, with fly.*

occupied by James Propert. It was in a building in the yard that the Cathedral Grammar School (ousted from Rock House) under its master Nathaniel Davies eventually settled during the 1840s. In 1854, Rev. Davies left for England and the school continued under Rev. Thomas Richardson until 1867. Grove House was shortly afterwards sold, and the school under its new master Rev. A. J. M. Green moved to Bryn-y-garn.

The former private residence and school became the first of the modern hotels in St. David's. It catered for the affluent visitors who were beginning to visit St. David's to view the cathedral, and those who came to study the wildlife and the world-famous geology of the area; Henry Hicks, one of the leading geologists of the time, was a local man. But William Williams was a man of vision; he catered for those who came to enjoy the bathing at Caerfai and Whitesands. He owned a considerable amount of land; he was tenant of Ramsey Island, and he held shooting rights over large areas of common land; he catered too for the sportsmen who came to enjoy the shooting and fishing. For their convenience he ran conveyances between the Grove Hotel and Haverfordwest Station. William Williams and his wife Martha were certainly hard working; they had to be. Of Mrs. Williams it was said that she had been known to leave the hotel, cross to Ramsey Island at 4 a.m., make 80 pounds of butter and be back in the Grove to prepare breakfast. On one occasion (according to Roscoe Howells) she was returning to the mainland with several tubs of butter, when a sudden wave caused one of the tubs to fall overboard. Nothing daunted, Mrs. Williams jumped in after it. One of her companions in the boat seized her by the hair, shouting: "Come here you silly old bugger!" Her reply was quoted as: "Never mind about me! Save the butter!" Her actual words were probably unrepeatable. Mrs. Williams survived; the fate of the butter is not recorded.

Perhaps that explains why when Francis Kilvert and his father visited St. David's in October 1871, they were informed by their driver that all the inns were "dirty and uncomfortable", and were advised to stay at the private house of "one Mr. Williams". The person with whom they stayed was George Owen Williams who then lived at New Cross.

To accommodate the influx of visitors other hotels were opened; among them the City Hotel in New Street, the Prospect Hotel in what was then Oakley Street and a few years later the Cross House Hotel. The promoter of the first was John Rees. Retired from the sea and living at Mynydd-ddu he had succeeded Samuel Williams as local Lloyd's Agent. His deputy was William Williams, the Grove. John Rees also became the Honorary Secretary of the St. David's Lifeboat in 1871 in succession to Dr. Henry Hicks.

Even today the City Hotel has the appearance of a railway hotel, which is precisely what it was intended to be. In 1870 there was a plan for a railway to link Haverfordwest to Fishguard via Treffgarne. It was the intention of the promoters, for whom Samuel Williams was correspondent to the press, to build a branch line from Heathfield to St. David's. The terminus was to be erected on what was then open land between Nun Street and New Street to the north of Town Hall Lane. The plan failed as the Haverfordwest and Fishguard Railway was never built. For many years the hotel stood in splendid isolation opposite the station that was not there for Dr. Beeching to close.

In February 1879 John Rees died and shortly afterwards the City Hotel was purchased by George Owen Williams. The Grove Hotel continued to prosper under William and Martha Williams for many more years. The former died in March 1899, and the family moved to Mynydd-ddu. The hotel was disposed of and the merchant business closed. The granaries were let to Adrian Owen Williams, merchant, of Old Cross. The wheel had turned full circle.

22. *The Grove Hotel; originally a private residence, later a school, it was converted to a hotel by William Williams.*

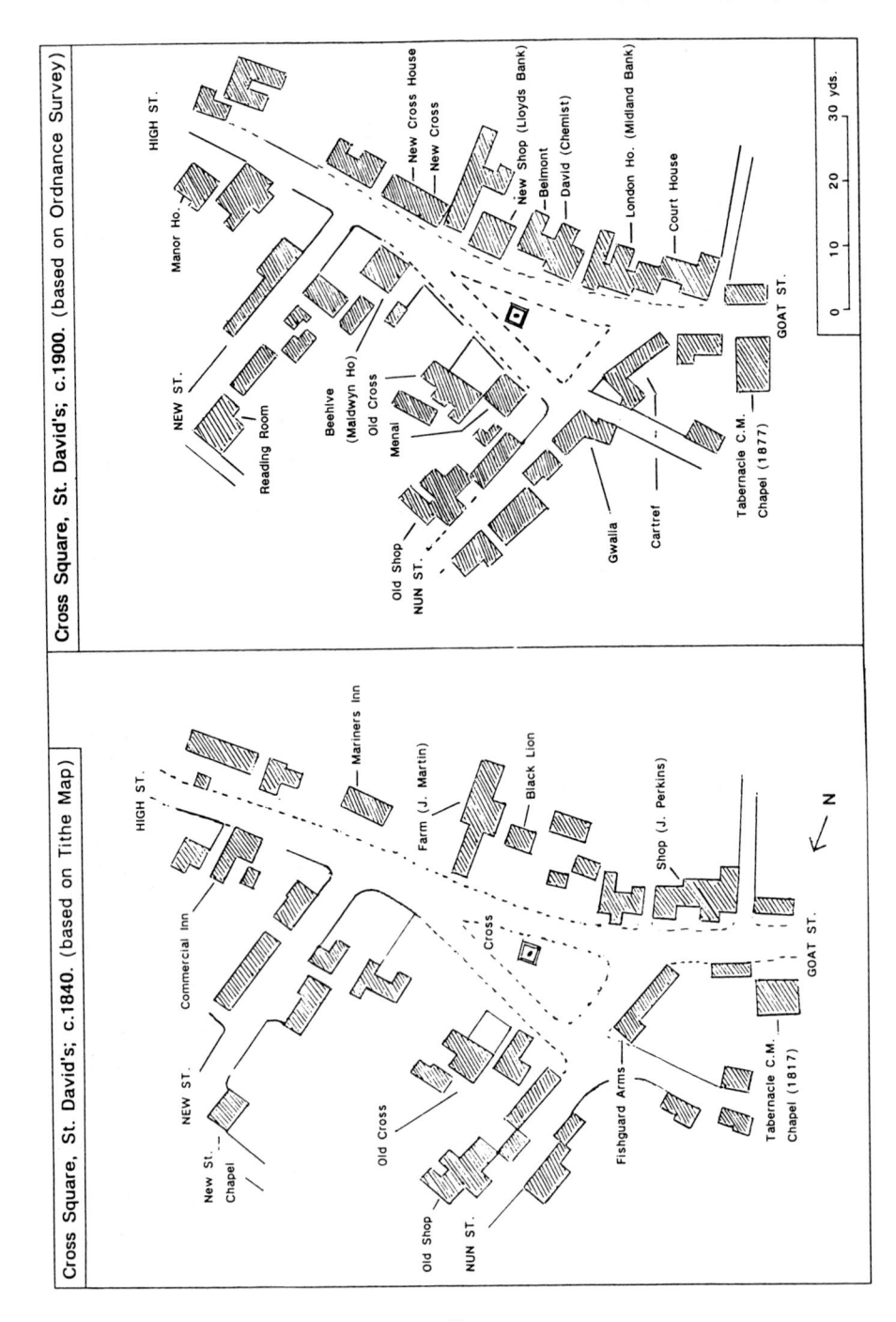

Cross Square, St. David's; c.1900. (based on Ordnance Survey)

Cross Square, St. David's; c.1840. (based on Tithe Map)

XII; About the Cross

The square, with its market cross, has always been the centre of everyday life in St. David's. From early Victorian times and for a hundred years, the land around the square was very much Williams territory. Here they had their homes; Old Cross and Menai (once known as Cross House) together occupied the northern side; on the southern side of High Street where it joins the square were the two houses called New Cross. There were other houses; on the southern side of the square Adrian Owen Williams owned Court House and the adjoining shop; at one time he also owned the two three-storeyed, semi-detached houses - London House (now Midland Bank) and Swn-y-don.

It was not always so; in 1840 Elizabeth Williams, widow, still lived at Old Shop with her children Samuel and Elizabeth. Her eldest son Ebenezer owned the schoolroom and cottages on the site of Menai; but that was the Old Shop family's only presence on the square. However, on the western side, in the oldest surviving house - dated 1778 - lived her nephew John Phillips. Still a young man he was to serve as Parish Clerk for more than half a century. Next door, on the site of Cartref, was a shop run by George Stephens and, on the corner, the Fishguard Arms kept by William Thomas; both were owned by Martha Griffiths.

Court House was then a shop owned and occupied by John Perkins. On the site of Midland Bank were several cottages owned by Henry Leach. Then, on either side of the lane came four cottages which were owned by Rev. Thomas Jones, the Wesleyan minister, who had married Elizabeth the daughter of William and Elizabeth Williams of Penlan. Where Belmont now stands was a large open space behind which were houses owned by Martha Williams of the Commercial Inn. The site of Lloyds Bank was a homestead owned and occupied by Henry Stephens who was also the Postmaster; formerly it had been the Black Lion. Beyond the little lane was a shop occupied by John Davies, and to the rear a homestead owned by John Harding Harries and occupied by John Martin. The site of New Cross was a garden and stable owned and occupied by William Harris of Hendre. Opposite, on the site of Barclays Bank was a garden owned by Dorothy Roberts and between that and Old Cross a shop owned by John Harding Harries and occupied by David Evan.

The only really substantial house on the square at that time was Old Cross. The many artists' impressions of the square made in the early nineteenth century invariably look towards the cathedral. They show the humble cottages and one or two slightly larger houses which lined the western side of the square and the upper end of Goat Street; some show the cottages which once stood on the north side of The Pebbles. Only the

23. Cross Square c.1825 showing part of Old Cross which then had a thatched roof; from a watercolour by Charles Norris.

later drawings show the recently built Fishguard Arms.

The other sides of the square are seldom shown; one exception is a watercolour by Charles Norris dating from about 1825. The view of the Market Cross from the south-east shows part of Old Cross which then had a thatched roof. The modern front lawn was a walled enclosure with a small building in one corner; like the house this appears to have been covered in brownish limewash. The site of Menai is occupied by small buildings, probably the schoolroom and cottages of the Tithe Map. Beyond is a much larger house which, from the map, would seem to be the domestic part of Old Shop. This, like all the other buildings had a thatched roof.

The original Old Cross, three-storeyed, with dormer windows, now forms the main part of the hotel. A later extension at the rear carried a stone dated 1766. Behind the house was an extensive range of outbuildings which are now incorporated in the hotel. In 1841 the house was owned by John Harding Harries and leased by William Harris of Hendre. The occupant for more than a decade had been Hester Harris, the latter's spinster daughter. At the time of the 1841 Census, Hester Harris, an 'Independent lady' was accompanied by her niece, the younger Elizabeth Owen. For the latter it was conveniently near the home of her sweetheart, Samuel Williams of Old Shop, whom she shortly afterwards married.

24. *A drawing of Cross Square as seen from the front of the Black Lion made in 1835 by Thomas Tudor.*

Ten years later, accompanied by a housekeeper, Hester Harris was still at Old Cross. Soon afterwards she moved to the newly-built New Cross. About this time Old Cross seems to have been purchased by Rev. William Watts Harris. After Miss Harris, Old Cross saw a number of occupants, most of whom stayed only briefly.

The house was empty in 1861, but in October 1862 it was occupied by Samuel Williams, newly returned from Liverpool. He later moved to Hendre and in March 1866 the house was vacant; a year later George Owen Williams was living there, but by September 1867 it was vacant again. In March 1868 it was being let on a monthly basis. It was once more vacant in October 1870, when Samuel Williams complained to the police authorities of windows being broken by local youths - Constable Pearce being then indisposed.

In 1871 the only occupant was Charles Thomas of Haverfordwest, a bailiff and described as visitor. By 1878 the occupier was John Harries Inkerman Williams, youngest of the three sons of Samuel and Elizabeth Williams. In 1881 he was living there with his Bristol-born wife Eunice and their two sons, but by 1886 they were living in 1, Grove Villas in High Street.

Mr. Inkerman Williams was replaced by his brother William Watts Williams, who was a widower with several small children. His wife

Martha was born in Hope Place in Liverpool, but her father Captain James Webb was a native of St. David's. The young couple lived for some years at Spring Gardens in High Street, but by 1871 they had moved to the imposing new farmhouse which had been built at Hendre. Two years later Mrs. Watts Williams died tragically in childbirth. William was left with four young children; Samuel, aged 7; Winifred, 5; Percy, 4; and Lilian who was just one year old.

At Old Cross William Watts Williams carried on business as a coal and general merchant, using the extensive range of outbuildings for the purpose. Like his father he was extremely active in chapel and community. When the Pembrokeshire County Council was created he was elected to represent St. David's. He later became an alderman; he played an important part in the running of the old Town Hall in New Street, and he was instrumental in the establishment of secondary education in St. David's. And it was the Town Hall which provided a temporary home to the school when it first opened in 1895. Ill-health eventually undermined his constitution and Mr. Watts Williams died in January 1899 at the age of only 54 years.

It was his younger daughter Lilian who became mistress at Old Cross after marrying her first cousin Adrian Owen Williams. There they remained for the rest of their days. Mr. Owen Williams carried on the business operated by his father-in-law, but it was as the member for St. David's on the County Council that he is best remembered.

Below Old Cross is the house now called Menai. Described by Cadw as a "Mid C19 substantial house in rusticated, unpainted stucco over rubble stone" it was originally built during the late 1840s as a shop by Ebenezer Williams, the druggist. Following his bankruptcy it was purchased by Rev. William Watts Harris, keeping it within the family.

The house was vacant in 1861, but afterwards it became a school run by Dr. Propert, who had earlier operated at Prospect House. The master did not believe in hiding his light under a bushel. In Kelly's Directory of 1906, then living in High Street, he is described as "Propert, William Peregrine, M.A., Ll.D., Mus.Bac., J.P., F.G.S., F.R.M.S., Barrister-at-law." At the time of the 1871 Census he was absent from home - the occupants were his 34 year old wife Emily, her two young sons and her spinster sister Elizabeth Mortimer who acted as housekeeper. There were also eight pupils. At the next census, Cross House contained Dr. Propert and his family together with six students. Later Dr. Propert moved with the school to Manor House in High Street.

The private school which had once been a chemist's shop next became a hotel. The Cross House Hotel was opened in 1887 by George and Mary Anne Williams who had left the City Hotel where they had been replaced by John and Frances Sime. Mr. Sime, a native of Huntly, Aberdeenshire, had moved to Pembrokeshire to become a farm bailiff at Kilpaison, near Rhoscrowther. Later he became a spirit merchant in Main Street, Pembroke, then a farmer at Arnold's Hill, Slebech, before moving to the City Hotel.

25. *A wintry scene in the 1890s of the Cross House Hotel and of Old Cross before it was obscured by trees.*

The visitors who came to Cross House included bishops and ministers, lecturers and professors, men of industry and commerce, naval officers and gentlefolk; even the football team from Neyland. One of the most notable, Rev. W. A. B. Coolidge described it:

> "The snug hostelry of the Cross House Hotel, which though itself modern (save as regards the old-fashioned hospitality of the good landlady) takes its name from the ancient market cross .... in the one piazza of the little city."

He came year after year, staying several weeks at a time, as did many others. Like most visitors he travelled in a primitive coach from the Salutation Inn at Haverfordwest, a long and uncomfortable journey. All were agreed on the comfort of the hotel and the welcome they received. The hotel continued for some eleven years, closing after the death of Mrs. Williams; the final signature in the visitors' book, dated 6th October, 1898, is that of Thomas Ellis of Aberystwyth.

George Owen Williams had no wish to continue the hotel. Meanwhile Samuel James Watts Williams of Old Cross had married and, on his father's death, succeeded to the Watts Harris property, including both Cross House and Old Cross. He and his wife (formerly Margaret John of

26. *Old Cross and Menai in the early years of the twentieth century.*

Beaumaris) settled in Cross House which was renamed Menai in her honour. So, in effect, the Watts Williams and the Owen Williams families exchanged houses.

The two houses known as the New Crosses were constructed in 1851 on land owned by Hester Harris and her sister Elizabeth Owen. Miss Harris took up occupation of Upper New Cross, and in 1861 was living there with one servant. Some time after her death in 1868 Samuel and Elizabeth Williams moved in and remained there until their deaths in 1891 and 1893 respectively. The house, not being part of the entailed estate, was left to their youngest son John Inkerman Williams. So the pattern was set for the next half century; Owen Williams of Old Cross, Watts Williams of Menai (Cross House) and Inkerman Williams of New Cross.

Lower New Cross had a much more chequered career. It was probably built for John and Elizabeth Owen, though they never settled there permanently. In 1861 it was unoccupied. Ten years later it was owned and occupied by George Owen Williams, though he soon afterwards moved to Lower Treginnis; the Williams family were notorious in the way in which they played musical chairs with their houses. Later he granted the house to his brother John.

27. *Cross Square from the east, early 1900s, after the introduction of gas street lighting, but before the enclosure of the City Green.*

"ROYAL MAIL" 1902   D.44

28. *Arrival of the Royal Mail, 1902, when the Post Office was located in New Cross.*

The house was then let. In 1881 the tenant was a Captain Griffiths; at the time of the census he was at sea and the house was occupied by his wife Martha and their four children. The house achieved a kind of fame as the 'Stone House' of *The Captain's Wife* by Eiluned Lewis which was based on the experiences of the family of her master-mariner grandfather. But, unlike many of the larger St. David's houses it was never the Captain's House.

The family was no longer there in 1891, when the sole occupant was 35 year old Martha James, a domestic servant. During the latter years of the century it became the home of Rev. William Jenkins, who was then minister of Tabernacle Chapel.

At the beginning of the new century the building housed the Post Office. The postmaster was Samuel Watts Williams, who had taken over from William Williams of Gwalia; his assistant was his cousin Lily Inkerman Williams. To provide access to the office an extra door was pierced in the front wall of the house; its outline is still discernable. However, within a few years the office moved to Court House.

Apart from Barclays Bank, reconstruction around the square was virtually complete by the beginning of the twentieth century. The thatched and whitewashed cottages had vanished and most had been replaced by sturdy Victorian houses and shops creating a new commercial centre.

First, except perhaps for Cross House, was a large house and shop erected in the 1840s on the site of cottages owned by Dorothy Roberts. It later became the Beehive, but in 1851 it was occupied by John Owen - a native of Milford - who was described as draper &c. Ten years later it was a grocers and drapers run by the unrelated George and Mary Ann Owen who were still there in 1891. By the latter half of the decade Maldwyn House (as it was then known) was the home of Frederick John Sime, registrar and relieving officer, and his wife Esther, daughter of George Owen and Mary Anne Williams. His parents had by this time left the City Hotel, where they had been replaced by the Arnolds, and had moved to the Swan Hotel which stood on Swan Square in Haverfordwest.

The year 1851 saw the building not only of New Cross but of two houses for John Harding Harries - the present Gwalia. The tenancy was taken up by William Williams (a member of the Rhoscribed family) who became postmaster and opened a drapery business. Mr. Williams purchased the property in 1857; later he was succeeded by his son William Davies Williams. In 1891 the latter was postmaster, his father lived in the adjoining house. Next door in Glendower, the first house in Nun Street, lived the unrelated William Wilfred Williams, L.R.C.P., M.R.C.S., the local doctor.

29. *Fred Sime and his surviving children, early 1920s: (rear), Nell (daughter-in-law), John, Hilda; (front), Lena, Muriel (with Billy), Lilian, Chrissie.*

The 1850s also saw the erection of two large houses on the site of the Black Lion. One was known as Dewi House, the other became a drapers known as the New Shop. The proprietors were John and Mary Owen, who had originally opened their business on the opposite side of the road. By the end of the century it was run by the Misses Owen who dealt mainly in fancy goods.

On the same side of the square, adjoining Goat Street, the shop once occupied by John Perkins had become The Druggist's House. In 1861 the occupier was Anne Hicks (widow of Dr. Thomas Hicks) who lived there with her three children, one of whom was the future Dr. Henry Hicks. Ten years later she had been replaced by the 25 years old pharmacist Henry Hughes, a native of Carmarthen, and his sister. By 1881 it was the chemist's shop of Albert David.

As late as 1890 the south side of the square between Lloyds Bank and Court House still retained the cottages which throughout the century had housed the agricultural labourer, the mariner, the tailor and the widowed dressmaker. All that was about to change.

In those last few years of the century Belmont was built and became the home of Captain Samuel Roach. A generous benefactor to St. David's, he was largely responsible for the erection during the 1920s of the modern City Hall in High Street which superseded the barn-like Old

30. Court House has probably changed little externally since Victorian times when it was the Druggist's House of Thomas and Anne Hicks.

Town Hall of Victorian days. Below Belmont the modern pharmacy was constructed by Albert David. Originally it was two houses, the upper of which became his shop. Finally the two houses, one of which is now Midland Bank, were erected as private residences by Thomas Thomas.

So the buildings that ring the square were complete. Since then there have been alterations to some of them, but they have been for the most part cosmetic. The most obvious changes have been to City Green in the centre of the square; that and the traffic that has replaced the horse and cart. In the second half of the twentieth century one building only has been significantly altered - Old Cross itself.

Were Samuel Roach and Albert David to return to St. David's nearly a century later they would undoubtedly recognise the Cross Square they knew. They would no doubt approve of the gardens, Captain Roach was one of the pioneers in that scheme, and in the replacement of the rutted tracks and open gutters with tidy streets and pavements. But whether they would approve all the changes is another matter.

St. David's

31. A remarkable aerial photograph of central St. David's from the south-east; it pre-dates the construction of the City Hall and Barclays Bank; perhaps the earliest such picture it is at the latest early 1920s.

XIII; 'Ratlin the Reefer'

On a calm summer's day in June 1870, the cliffs around St. Non's Bay were thronged with spectators. On the most prominent point - the topmast - stood Ratlin the Reefer himself; with him were his cronies Top Bowline, Clew line and Bunt line. They, and the others, had come to watch the St. David's Regatta, and in particular the long-awaited contests between the lifeboats of Solva and St. David's, both of which had only entered service the previous year.

The *Dewsland and Kemes Guardian* of Saturday, June 25th, contains a (largely factual) account of the event. In the rowing race the St. David's lifeboat *Augusta*, coxswain Captain Hicks, had defeated the Solva lifeboat *Charles & Mary Egerton*, coxswain Captain Lloyd, by 100 yards. In the sailing race which was marred by a lack of wind the same boat had triumphed by a quarter of a mile.

The first of the other races, a four-oared race for boats under 24 feet was won by *Bonetta*, owned by Samuel Williams, coxed by G. Owen Williams; second was the Solva boat *Water Witch*, owned by J. R. J. Nash, coxed by A. Woollett; with *Mary* in third place and *Emily* last. The two-oared race for boats under 20 feet was won by *Water Witch* with *Ferret* second and *Lively* third. A sculling race was won by the young lad John Thomas in *Lively*, with John Watt in *Mary* second and Capt. George Lile in *Otter* ignominiously last. In a novelty Duck Hunt, the hunters in *Bonetta* chased after William Narbet in *Ferret*. "Duck having found that green peas were not plentiful just at present, declined to be seized and overhauled."

The final event, an open race, saw another confrontation between the white-painted *Water Witch* and the black *Bonetta*, which this time had W. Watts Williams as coxswain.

"The excitement on shore was intense, and as either 'white' or the 'black' seemed to be gaining an advantage, up and down went the 'trot' and 'lump' thermometers, and when after some ten minutes the *Bonetta* passed the flag boat first, we heard several grave expressions rather unfavourable to 'yr hen cwch du', but never mind the tables may and very likely will be changed next time. Cheer up Solva folk, though your star was not in the ascendant this time, yet, on your own waters, and possibly after divesting yourselves of any over confidence that you may possess, you will yet see our St. David's Cousins go home more chop-fallen than exultant."

The paper also announced that the next edition would contain some 'Rambling Reflections' on the regatta by 'Ratlin the Reefer'. These begin with a lengthy tongue-in-cheek introduction advising against excessive blarney, followed by a warning to the St. David's men that: "although they carried off the honours of the day, yet they ought not to be too boastful." He continues:

> "First of all, Life Boats. We scanned them with our clove hitched eye, and put down at once St. David's as the winner. Why? Because it was more trim and in better rowing order; the Solva boat has not sufficient ballast on board, and therefore rows in an unsteady manner. It cannot be otherwise while she is in her present trim, and that we are right was evidently and palpably proved by the stroke the Solva crew pulled after taking in such a number of passengers for home. We confess that their strokes then were by far the best of the day, and we believe that had the *Charles & Mary Egerton* 5cwt. more ballast in her she would have 'licked' the *Augusta*. She is the more powerful boat, and ought, and will win ere long, crew for crew. The sailing match was not a fair one, the Solva boat ought not to have allowed the St. David's one to have gone to windward, it being so far preventable that our companions on the yard, topbowline &c., and selves, agreed that it was a complete sell and 'Mother carey' of the race and result. Then again, Solva was 'abroad' as to tide, all the stream running east at that most particular time, so the shore ought to have been 'hugged' and this was advantageously seen from our topsail yard when St. David's pretty nigh entered 'John Martin's Chambers', thereby having all the benefit of a westward ho! eddy, Solva the while was out in the very strength and ripple of an eastward current. Read, mark and learn, Solva. Sit down quietly and cogitate, you have been 'beat' so goes the word, but not for want of pluck, energy or power, but by a little, very little wee bit of 'over confidence' in yourselves and the want of judgment in trimming your boat. You row well, you did row well that day, but you rowed best when you had cooled down and the 'shine' had been taken out of you, fact is you had made up your mind to have all your own way, and suddenly when you realized that St. David's was alongside with an inkling of heading you, you got flurried, 'thrashed oats as they do in Dewsland' and got 'flabergasted', 'licked', 'chawed up', &c., &c."

The other events were treated in a similar jocular manner. In the four-oared race Top-bow had selected *Water Witch* as the likely winner, Clew chose *Bonetta* and Bunt favoured *Mary*. When challenged, Ratlin replied deliberately: "I will not say *Emily*." The skill of the stroke in *Bonetta* proved decisive; the result was summed up as: "1 System, 2 Exertion, 3 Strength, 4 Hardiness."

The two-oared race proved disastrous for *Lively* due to Mr. Watts

Williams choosing a steering oar much too long for such a small craft. The sculling race was equally disastrous for Captain Lile who lost his hat and came down "like a 'thousand of bricks' ", to the amusement of all. The Duck Race was a procession, notable only for the unseemly behaviour of the quarry.

The result of the last race was also described as unfair; *Water Witch* should have won: "the owner of Black even despairing of his boat." *Water Witch* is described as: "a pretty boat, pretty enough to send a thrill through any one owning a boat to oppose her, but she has not the rising power necessary for a match boat." There was talk of a return match, proposed by Samuel Williams and Captain John Davies, to be held at Solva during August, when it was hoped the Fishguard and Milford (as the Angle boat was then known) lifeboats would also compete. Meanwhile: "St. David's look out, there are squalls about."

In Victorian times correspondents to the local press frequently wrote under assumed names. Who then was 'Ratlin the Reefer'? The letter books of Samuel Williams supply the answer. For there are to be found the two accounts which later appeared in the paper. The pseudonym of 'Ratlin the Reefer' was but one of many adopted by Mr. Williams who

32. *George Owen Williams aboard the family boat.*

wrote on a variety of topics: religion, education, the railway project, trade, and many others, both anonymously and under his own name.

The writer was himself the owner of *Bonetta* which had seen off the Solva challenge. He could poke gentle fun at the Solva lifeboatmen who had attempted to sail directly across the bay, while their St. David's rivals had used their superior local knowledge of the currents to outwit their opponents by creeping close inshore under the cliffs. No doubt the account began many an argument in the Cambrian and the Ship in Solva and in the Mitre and the Farmers in St. David's during the following weeks.

Why the reference to 'trots' and 'lumps' - who were they? Like the Haverfordwest 'longnecks' - a name still remembered, the St. David's 'trots' (or 'trotters') and the Solva 'lumps' were the nicknames given to the inhabitants of those places. 'The Chambers' are caves at the north-eastern corner of St. Non's Bay and the fields above were owned by John Martin who lived on Cross Square. And 'thrashed oats as they do in Dewsland' speaks for itself.

Although he had not himself taken part in the regatta, Samuel Williams still remained an active sailor. In a letter dated 9th December, 1870, to his nephew George Perkin Williams on board ship in China, he reminisces how George and John Francis (who had recently died of smallpox) had climbed after gulls' eggs on Ramsey Island:

PUFFINS.

33. Puffins on North Bishop, photographed by George Owen Williams.

"I can see you now up Allt felyn fawr ..... so high up. I could not look at you sometimes you went so high and through such dangerous places. I would not take ten thousand pounds to do what you both did ..... that day."

Since George had left home they had continued fishing and climbing after birds. More recently they had tried to catch seals - without success. The couple they had netted had managed to escape. The crew of another boat, who had larger nets, had captured four seals. Next year Samuel hoped to fish more extensively and make a profit.

Meanwhile there was work to be done; *Bonetta* was still afloat at the quay, she must be taken out of the water to dry out. The boat needed painting and there were timbers to be replaced. There were new nets to be made and old ones to be mended. There was plenty to occupy Samuel Williams and his man Billy Davies before the next summer, when perhaps there would be another meeting with *Water Witch*.

XIV; Wreck of the *Prince Cadwgan*

During the early hours of Saturday, 30th September, 1876, the 83 ton screw steamer *Prince Cadwgan* was making her way westward along the coast from Solva towards Ramsey Sound. The ship was on the return leg of her fortnightly voyage between her home port of Aberaeron and Bristol; she had unloaded some 20 tons of cargo at Solva and was making for Fishguard her next port of call.

The night was dark, but on the bridge the ship's master, 50 years old Thomas Evans, an experienced mariner, was confident in his knowledge of this hazardous coast. Also on the bridge, and at the wheel, was the mate Evan Evans aged 44. On the forecastle were two seamen; Evan Pugh, at 68 much the oldest of the crew, and David Jones who was twenty years his junior. The remaining members of the crew; the 24 years old engineer Thomas Roberts and two stokers; David Lott and John Davies (aged respectively 44 and 24) were below in the engine-room. Apart from the engineer, who came from Aberystwyth, all the crew hailed from Aberaeron.

The report of the master on the events which followed is contained in the *Cambrian News* of Friday, 12th October:

"September 30th, 2 a.m., got steam up and proceeded wind E. to S.E. light, hazy. 2.20 a.m. mate at helm and 2 men on forecastle, master on bridge. Mate called out: 'Breakers ahead'. Directed helm to be put hard to starboard; 5 minutes afterwards engineer to drive faster ahead when he reported blades of propellor broken by striking rock. Engines were then stopped. At 2.30 a.m. tide three-quarters flood weather hazy, wind E. to S.E. light breeze with ground swell from westard. The ship in consequence of her way having been stopped and the wind on port bow fell with her broadside right on the west side of Crow Rock, quarter mile from mainland near end of Ramsey Sound and knocked a hole in her bottom when she filled with water and soon after sank in 2 fathoms. The ship's boat having been got out she was left in that state and stranded about 10 minutes after she struck. 3 a.m. Crew landed in safety at Porthlisky Harbour."

The unfortunate *Prince Cadwgan* had been the pride of Aberaeron. Built at Glasgow in 1864 she had since then operated a regular service between Aberaeron and Bristol, serving also the ports of North Pembrokeshire. She was the first steamship to trade between Cardigan Bay and Bristol, though paddle-steamers like the ill-fated *Frolic* and the *County of Pembroke* had been sailing from Bristol to Milford and Haverfordwest since 1830. The owners of the *Prince Cadwgan* were the

34. The Prince Cadwgan *(extreme left) at Bristol in 1868; the other steamers are the* Dolphin *and* Druid.

Aberayron Steam Navigation Co. Ltd., most of the shareholders being local shopkeepers; in 1876 the managing director was John H. Jones of Anchor House, Aberaeron.

The survivors were taken to Lower Treginnis where they were provided with food and shelter. The captain then returned to the scene of the wreck along with the farmer George Owen Williams. Here they were joined by the coastguard and a number of other local men. Carreg Fran is linked to the mainland by a rocky reef which is exposed at low tide and the men were able to scramble over this to reach the wreck. It was immediately obvious that nothing could be done to save the ship, and Captain Evans directed the men to salvaging the cargo. He then returned to the mainland with the coastguard - a man who had only taken up his post at St. David's the previous day - in order to make an official statement.

Here they met Samuel Williams on his way to the wreck. The Lloyd's Agent and the local Receiver of Wrecks were both away from home. Mr. Williams, who was Receiver of Wrecks for the coast north of Ramsey Sound, and was a former Lloyd's Agent, was deputed by the captain to take charge of salvage operations.

By midday a considerable amount of the cargo (according to one account two-thirds) had been landed on the rocks. Throughout the afternoon the wind increased and a heavy swell swept most of the salvaged cargo from the rocks before it could be taken to the mainland. During the storm the *Prince Cadwgan* herself slipped off the rocks and foundered in thirty feet of water.

By this time the rising tide and the wind made it impossible for the twenty or so men on the island to get to shore, nor was it possible to reach them by boat from Porthclais. They were condemned to spend the night without shelter, warmth or light on Carreg Fran, which, barely an acre in extent, was lashed by torrential rain and drenching spray. They spent a long and miserable night; cold, hungry and thirsty, huddled together on the exposed rock. Meanwhile, captain and crew slept soundly in the warm, comfortable beds of Lower Treginnis.

The following morning, when the tide had receded and the wind moderated, Captain Evans returned to the island. With the agreement of Captain John Rees - the Agent for Lloyd's and also the local Agent for the steamship company - who had by now arrived on the scene, it was decided that Samuel Williams should continue to direct salvage operations. Owing to the weather conditions however little could be done other than to remove what was left to higher ground on the island. The bad weather continued almost unabated and on 13th October - a fortnight after the shipwreck - only 19 bolts of canvas and some wine had been brought to the mainland as reported to the Board of Trade by Mr. Williams.

Only when all the immediate salvage operations were complete did the Customs Officer, Charles Brown of Solva - he held the official position of tidewaiter at Solva and also at Porthclais - appear. He at once assumed responsibility of the operations and took credit for all that had been done; as a result the term "Brown's Salvage" was for some time a byword in the neighbourhood.

Captain Evans and his crew remained at Treginnis during the attempts at salvage. They were well looked after by the lady of the house Mary Anne Williams, who was accustomed to taking paying guests at the farm, and her eleven year old daughter Esther. Particularly grateful for their kindness was one member of the crew who had become indisposed as a result of the wreck and was confined to bed for several days. Captain Evans had a son Thomas who was about the same age as Esther Williams; he was anxious that the two children should meet, though, as far as is known, they never did.

The two families maintained contact for some time. Captain Evans returned to sea and it became his habit when he passed Treginnis to sound a blast on his ship's siren. Later George Owen Williams left the farm for the City Hotel in St. David's and the link was broken.

Esther Williams eventually married Frederick John Sime whose family were then running the Swan Hotel in Haverfordwest. They had seven children, but only one son - John Alexander. After serving in the First World War he became a student at St. David's College, Lampeter. There he met and fell in love with and eventually married Nell Evans, the daughter of a sea captain. As a girl she had twice accompanied her father in the sailing ship *Howth* on voyages around the world. Her father, Thomas Evans, was the son of Thomas Evans of Aberaeron, master of the *Prince Cadwgan*.

The two families did come together, albeit a generation later.

35. *Roy and Mary Harris view the scene of the wreck of the* Prince Cadwgan *which foundered on the near side of Carreg Fran — the further island. Mrs. Harris is the daughter of John and Nell Sime and great granddaughter of George Owen Williams of Treginnis and of Captain Thomas Evans of the* Prince Cadwgan.

XV; Tragedy at Treginnis

"The Jury find that the deceased, John Reynolds, fell out of a certain tub in a certain copper mine at Treginnis, and so died of the injuries thereof; and that the Jury strongly disapprove of the conduct of the four men engaged with the deceased at the said works."

So ran the verdict at the inquest on John Reynolds, who died following an accident which occurred at the copper mine on Wednesday, 2nd May, 1883. With the accident ended mining at Lower Treginnis, an enterprise which had begun with such high hopes many years previously.

The Treginnis Copper Mine had apparently been opened about 1827. The original proprietors were two brothers, James and John Stephens, who were natives of Scotland. They had obtained a lease from the landowner, Henry Harries, to work the minerals under the property.

They began their operations at Penmaenmelyn, where veins of copper ore had been discovered. The ruined buildings and shafts of their enterprise can still be seen on an artificial shelf cut into the cliff on the shores of Ramsey Sound directly opposite the Bitches. Early promises of success were not fulfilled. The copper-bearing lodes soon petered out, and, in spite of much searching, could not be found again. The brothers money ran out, and within a few years the project was abandoned.

For years the mine lay neglected and largely forgotten. Henry Harries died in 1851 and the farm and mine passed to his relation Samuel Williams. In 1856 Lower Treginnis was put up to be auctioned on Tuesday, 1st July; in the advertisement no mention is made of the mine. However the sale was postponed until Thursday, 10th July; this time the notice in the *Haverfordwest and Milford Haven Telegraph* contains the following addition:

"The attention of the Public is particularly drawn to the COPPER MINES which are supposed to lie under this property. A considerable outlay has already been made in sinking shafts with a view to working them."

The property was bought by Thomas Llewellin, a bachelor, who lived there in the style of a gentleman farmer until his death in 1871 when the farm was sold. The purchaser was George Owen Williams, son of the previous owner. He had lived at Treginnis as a young boy, and he and his brother William would undoubtedly have explored the old mine at Penmaenmelyn. He had always been keenly interested in science, particularly nature study and geology, and very likely his interest in the mine played a significant part in his decision to purchase the farm.

One of his first acts was to have a geological survey of Lower Treginnis made by Dr. Percy of the Royal School of Mines. The results were sufficiently encouraging for him to consider selling the mineral rights of the farm. Discussions were held with several interested parties; these proved inconclusive and Mr. Williams decided to work the mine for himself.

His operations were centered on a shaft at Porth Taflod. Here, a quarter of a mile south of the original mine at Penmaenmelyn, the prospects for success seemed greatest. And here were gathered on the fateful morning the five men then employed at the mine. John Reynolds of Solva, John Rees of Middle Mill, Thomas Llewellyn of Clegyrfwya and John Price had worked at the mine for several months. For Henry Tegan it was his second day. The mineowner was by then living at the City Hotel, and the farm tenant was David Arnold who was also present at the mine for part of the morning.

The shaft was about thirty feet deep. A bucket, attached by a rope to a hand-operated winch standing to one side of the shaft, was used to haul men and materials to the surface. The rope ran over a pulley which was suspended from a wooden tripod erected over the shaft. The normal practice adopted by a miner was to stand with one foot in the bucket, using the other to steady himself against the wood-lined side of the shaft, while grasping the rope above his head.

36. *The depression in the ground marks the site of the shaft at Porth Taflod, scene of the fatal accident at the Treginnis Copper Mine.*

It was mid morning before the men entered the workings; on that particular day the task was to blast rock in one of the tunnels. First to be lowered was Llewellyn, followed by Rees; both were let down in the normal manner. A call from the men below demanded another man to join them to load the bucket with rubble to be brought to the surface. It was Reynolds who joined them; apparently it was his turn to work down the mine.

Unlike the others, Reynolds did not adopt the normal posture in the bucket. Perhaps from fear he invariably stood with both feet inside the bucket, and he did not grip the rope as high as did the rest. This made the bucket less stable and more inclined to sway. He reached the bottom safely, though when the bucket touched ground it, perhaps not surprisingly, toppled over. This was reported by Arnold who hinted that Reynolds had been let down more rapidly than the others.

About 1 p.m. preparations were complete and arrangements were made for the men to return to the surface. It was decided that Reynolds should be the first to ascend. He was raised a few feet, before being lowered again. He was settled once more into the bucket and for a second time winched upwards. When he was about half way to the surface there was a sudden jerk on the rope and Reynolds plunged to the bottom of the shaft.

He was obviously badly injured. John Rees rendered what aid he could; Reynolds was strapped into the bucket and cautiously raised to the surface. Dr. James was immediately summoned from St. David's and the injured man was carried to the City Hotel. Here a closer examination showed that he had suffered a broken neck, and was almost totally paralysed.

On the following day Reynolds expressed a desire to make a deposition. This was taken during the afternoon, in the presence of Dean Allen (a Justice of the Peace); Mr. W. Vaughan James, clerk to the magistrates; Dr. James; Sergeant Irvine of Solva; Constable John James; Henry Tegan and John Price.

In his sworn statement John Reynolds described the layout at the shaft and the events leading up to the accident. He continued:

"I went into the box a second time. I was standing up. The box then stopped going up and they jerked me. ....(They) threatened (me) because I said they were breaking my pick .... and (they said) I was no friend of theirs. I blame John Price and Henry Tegan for my fall .... they were driving the gear too fast, the drum too fast."

Although his mind remained relatively clear there was no hope of recovery and John Reynolds died on the morning of Friday, 4th May. He left a widow and two young children. The inquest was held at the City Hotel on the following Monday and adjourned until Thursday, 17th May, to allow for the attendance of a member of the Inspectorate of Mines.

At the resumed inquest, H.M. Inspector of Mines, Mr. E. W. Randall, described how he had visited the mine and examined the machinery. The system was, he said, very old fashioned but he could find no serious fault. He considered it most likely that the druke (axle) had come out of its bearing as a result of Reynolds falling from the box. He had suggested some simple modifications to prevent this happening again; the mineowner had agreed to implement these.

The miners were in turn examined by the Coroner, Capt. O. T. Edwardes, and answered (sometimes pointed) questions put by members of the Jury. All denied that they had in any way tampered with the machinery, or attempted to play practical jokes on the deceased.

In his summing up, the Coroner instructed the Jury that if the men - Price and Tegan - had interfered with the machinery they would be guilty of manslaughter; but, if there had been malicious intent it would be murder. However, he seemed satisfied that the miners had spoken the truth. The Jury was less convinced, and, after lengthy deliberations and further discussions with the Coroner, brought in their verdict.

That was not the end of the story. *The Dewsland and Kemes Guardian* for 6th June reported that John Price and Henry Tegan had appeared before James Brown Esq. M.P. on the previous Monday at the Shire Hall, Haverfordwest, charged with the manslaughter of John Reynolds. Each was remanded on bail of £100, with two sureties of £50 to answer the charge at Mathry Courthouse on the following Friday.

The charge had been brought at the instigation of Phebe Reynolds, the victim's widow. The defendants pleaded "Not guilty" and were discharged. The two men walked free from the Court, but the stigma remained with them for the rest of their lives. The Treginnis Copper Mine was never reopened.

XVI; 'Sion Bob Ochr'

It was Samuel Williams who, in a Supplement to the *Dewsland and Kemes Guardian*, dated Saturday, 21st January, 1871, used the term "Sion bob ochr" referring to himself; and it was he who translated it as "Jack of all sides". The purpose of the Supplement was to make available information which he, as chairman, had provided to a public meeting held during the previous month on the topic of education in St. David's. He attributed his appointment as chairman to the fact that he numbered members of all the different sects among his friends.

"They think that I am of the same religious opinions as themselves, and the consequence is that this one, that, and the other of the Independents have often told me 'you are a Congregationalist in secret, were you to confess the truth.' Many a Baptist has also told me right confidentially 'you are of the same opinion as us, and with us you will be ere long.' A Wesleyan believes, and tells me so 'You are a Wesleyan since childhood but you are rather shy so far to confess it.' There has not been a week passed since a Churchman (and he holds office among his brethren) 'you are (said he) more than three quarters of a Churchman. I know that (he said) and every Sunday I expect to see you coming to Church, where you ought to be.' The latter part was spoken in a very authoratative tone but with a patronising mien. Whilst the poor Methodists make a greater mistake than all the others by saying 'Oh, he is only half a Methodist.' "

But as he said he was not what the English called a "milk and water character". He had been chosen not because he was a "Jack of all sides", but because he was a "Jack without a side." He was a man who held strong opinions, but respected for all that. He was, and always had been a fervent advocate for the provision of education by the state. It was the Church which originally supported state education, while the Nonconformists, fearing government intervention, opposed it. Later the positions were reversed, but Samuel could boast that his position had not changed. During the 1870s two schools were built on Quickwell Hill; the Board School and the Church or National School. Samuel Williams was elected as the first chairman of the St. David's School Board.

Samuel Williams had been a Presbyterian Methodist all his life. His wife Elizabeth Owen had been brought up in the Established Church. After her marriage, as usually happened in such cases, she became a member of Tabernacle like her husband; all the children were raised as members of that chapel. But religious differences still ran deep and it was almost certainly these which on one occasion almost brought about

37. *Y Bont once housed one of the old private schools of St. David's. The old Carding Mill is visible beyond Pont y Penyd in this late nineteenth century photograph.*

separation of husband and wife. Samuel threatened to leave St. David's for ever, but reason prevailed and they were reconciled.

The predominant language of the home, like that of the chapel, was Welsh, But Samuel, like most of the Williamses was truly bilingual. He had, after all, been partly educated in Bristol and he had spent several years as a ship-broker in Liverpool; in any case English was the language of commerce. The thousands of letters he wrote were almost invariably in English; not only those dealing with business, but those to family and friends who were Welsh speaking. In his later years he often read his Bible late into the night, comparing the English and Welsh versions, sometimes favouring one, sometimes the other. True to character he described himself in the census of 1891 as monoglot Welsh.

After his return from Liverpool, Samuel assumed control of the estates which his wife had inherited from her uncle. He resumed his commercial operations as a general merchant, though on a much reduced scale; his fleet now consisted of only one small sailing vessel. He could really have lived on the rents from the estate, but he could not bear to be idle. He was able to devote much of his time to his various interests in and around St. David's. This was particularly the case when he retired from active life and the day to day running of the estate and the merchant business was taken over by his son William Watts Williams.

It was in the field of education that his efforts bore greatest fruit. Having himself received the benefits of a good schooling, he was a fervent advocate of elementary education for all. There were during the 1860s good schools in St. David's; the Cathedral Grammar School under Thomas Richardson at the Grove; the private school of W. P. Propert in Cross House; and there was a school for girls in the Close. But they were chiefly schools for boarders, for the children of the clergy and the minor gentry. For the rest there were only schools such as that run in 1861 by the 64 years old schoolmistress Miss Mary Appleby who lived in Priskilly Terrace.

Elections for the School Board held on 13th March, 1871, resulted in Samuel Williams being elected together with Rev. Thomas Jones, William Martin of Trehenlliw, Richard Williams of Penberry and Ebenezer Rees of Tremynydd. On 31st March Mr. Williams was appointed as chairman with Rev. Jones as vice chairman. A seat on the Board was no sinecure, particularly for the chairman who also dealt with the correspondence. A site for the school had to be purchased and plans drawn up for its construction. A building contractor must be appointed and his work supervised. There was furniture and equipment to be purchased and a master to be engaged before the school could open. Then there was another school to be built at Carnhedryn.

It was a period of much activity in St. David's, and Samuel had a part in much of what was happening. It was a time of restoration in the Cathedral and of the construction of the new Tabernacle Chapel in which the Williams family played an important part. It was a time when many of the large houses of St. David's were built; Lawn Villa and Hendre by the Williams family; Cathedral Villas in Nun Street by Captain John Davies; Glasfryn, on the site of 'The Old Windmill', by Dr. Henry Hicks. There were many more, large and small. And for the benefit of the general public a Reading Room was established in New Street on the site of the first Presbyterian Methodist Chapel and, for concerts and lectures, the Old Town Hall which is now the Catholic Church of St. Michael.

The chairman at many of the lectures and debates at the Town Hall was Samuel Williams. He was a member of many of the public bodies of the day. He was one of the leading members of the committee formed to promote the St. David's Railway project, for which he acted as secretary. He was a fervent supporter of Temperance and led many of the public meetings on the topic which were held in the Town Hall.

Samuel Williams was for many years a deacon at Tabernacle, who knew and corresponded with almost every Presbyterian minister in Wales; the bulk of which correspondence was only matched by that on maritime affairs with masters and owners of ships and with merchants throughout the country. It was he who drew up an ornately decorated letter in multi-coloured inks - a letter from the inhabitants of St. David's to the House of Commons petitioning against the sale of intoxicating liquor. A copy is to be found in one of Samuel Williams' Letter Books. A few pages away is another addressed to Mr. George Bennett, Spirit Merchant of Fishguard:

"... having heard that you have some very good Rum on sale will you be kind enough to send me one gallon of your best as it is wanted for a particular purpose medicinally."

Samuel Williams was indeed a man of many parts. Even in his later years after he had retired from active life he continued to follow the movements of vessels and to report these to interested parties. From his room, light would stream far into the night as he wrote letters appealing for assistance on behalf of the poor, or to masters of ships for mothers seeking news of their sons. He died at New Cross on 28th October, 1891, aged 72. As was said in his obituary.

"There was but one Mr. Samuel Williams."

38. *The cottages at the Merrivale were typical of many in St. David's at the end of the nineteenth century, but few shared their idyllic setting.*

XVII; Martyrs of the Faith

"In memory of JOHN LLOYD WILLIAMS of St. David's and London, who died on March 19th, 1900 aged 50 years. Also of ELIZABETH, his sister, and her husband HERBERT DIXON, both Martyrs of the Faith in China, August, 1900."

These few words carved on a tombstone in the windswept cemetery high above the River Alun commemorate an almost forgotten tragedy which took place halfway around the world nearly a century ago.

The *Haverfordwest and Milford Haven Telegraph* of 20th June, 1855, contained the announcement of the birth of a daughter to the wife of Thomas Williams of Cross Square, St. David's. Thomas Williams was the only son of John Williams who farmed at Clegyr Isaf; his wife Elizabeth - after whom the baby was named - was the younger daughter of George Williams of the Old Shop. The couple were first cousins and, like the rest of the family, were steeped in the Presbyterian tradition.

Thomas Williams was, like his father, a farmer; he also took over the lease of the windmill which had previously been held by his father-in-law. But when the young Elizabeth was still an infant the family left St. David's and moved to Cardiff where two of Thomas's sisters had already settled.

While in Cardiff, Mr. Williams helped to establish Salem Chapel in Canton. Among the founder members was another former member of Tabernacle Chapel, Mr. David Evans who had been brought up at Porthmawr. He later returned to St. David's and strangely purchased the windmill which he continued to operate until the early years of the twentieth century. He later converted this to a hotel, and he also developed the City Stores and City Bakery in High Street and was instrumental in forming the St. David's Gas and Water Company.

After several years spent in Cardiff and Liverpool, Thomas Williams also returned to St. David's where he became a farm bailiff. For a time he lived in Goat Street, later moving to Spring Gardens and finally to Mount Pleasant. The younger Elizabeth, perhaps influenced by the years she spent in the large and developing cities, did not remain long in her birthplace. In 1874, and not yet twenty years old, she set out for London. It was a journey which was to lead to adventure, to romance and eventually to a terrible death.

In the succeeding years Elizabeth met and married Herbert Dixon who was a Baptist minister. With him she had travelled to China where they became Christian missionaries. Between 1886 and 1891 they had four children; Benjamin, Charles, Mary and Ridley. While the children were young Elizabeth returned to Britain to look after them at home in

39. *A family group of the Dixons taken before Herbert and Elizabeth returned to China for the last time. The children are (from left): Ridley, Charles, Mary, Benjamin.*

Cambridge.

By the late 1890s the children were old enough to be left in boarding school and to spend their holidays with family and friends. Rev. Dixon had come home on leave and when he returned to China his wife accompanied him. On their way they had stopped in South Africa where the Dixons had relatives. In a letter home to her aunts Mrs. Ann Evans and Miss Sarah Williams at Harbour House in Solva, Elizabeth commented: "But what very troubled times they are having there now." Little did she realise what fate held in store for her husband and herself.

The mission settlement where the Dixons lived was at Hsin Chou, a town situated to the east of the large city of Tai Juan and some 250 miles south-west of Pekin. It was April 1900 and Elizabeth was able to describe the spacious premises they occupied, where, since her return from Britain, she had opened a small boarding-school for young Chinese girls at which they were taught the Christian faith; there was already a flourishing boys' school. There was a garden where she could grow flowers and vegetables, and sometimes she would accompany her husband on horseback on his visits to the outlying villages. It was a letter full of hope - she even invited her cousin Henry to come to visit her.

On his travels Rev. Dixon almost always carried a gun. It was not for protection but to shoot game birds - duck, partridge and bustard - for the pot. During the winter months he had shot a number of wolves and foxes; the skins of the former were being made into rugs.

But storm clouds were already gathering in the form of the Boxers, a secret society dedicated to driving out or killing all foreigners and Christians. By early June they had taken over Pao ting fu, a city east of Hsin Chou, thereby cutting off the missions at the latter and at Tai Juan from the coast. Worse was to follow! Towards the end of the month the mission at Tai Juan was attacked and set on fire by the insurgents; one at least of the missionaries was burnt to death, the remainder forced into hiding.

The arrival of the Boxers at Hsin Chou could not be long delayed. Swift action was essential if the Dixons and their fellow missionaries were to escape. A council was held and the eight missionaries - four men and four women - decided they must leave the city immediately and make for the hills to the south-west where they could hide from their pursuers until helped arrived.

Loading what they could onto carts they made good their escape and eventually reached the home of a Christian family. To remain there was impossible as it was the first place the pursuing Boxers would look, but at least they could arrange for help from other Christians.

The remainder of the day was spent hiding in a gully, where most of their possessions were then buried. After darkness had fallen other Christians arrived to guide them into the mountains. The ladies riding on horseback or on donkeys, the men mostly on foot, the nightmare journey began. Not daring to speak or to show a light, they stumbled, now through water, now through deep sand, at times losing touch with their guides, until at last they reached the entrance to a narrow pass. Then came a hazardous ascent over a rocky path which led deeper into the mountains.

Daylight found them near a village which they dared not enter for fear of being discovered. All day they lay hidden in a hollow, drenched by torrential rain. After dark they were taken to the village where the ladies were hidden in a cellar while the men were escorted to a nearby cave for the night.

For several days they remained in the village, during which time messengers were despatched to try to reach the coast to inform the authorities of their plight and to beg for assistance to be sent. Meanwhile the news they received was extremely serious. At Tai Juan all the missionaries and their families had been rounded up and imprisoned. From Hsin Chou the Boxers were setting out to hunt down the fugitives.

To leave the village was imperative. Another trying overnight march followed; their destination a tiny cave hollowed out of the hillside, barely large enough to hold them. There was no water nearby, their own supplies were running out, and the food which the villagers could supply was pitifully meagre and unpalatable. In any case the Christian Chinese were in just as great danger. By day they must lie quietly within the cave, huddled together on their soaking wet bedding; only at night dared they venture forth. The news they received could hardly have been worse. At Tai Juan the European missionaries, Catholic and Protestant, men, women and children, altogether nearly forty in number, had been put cruelly to death. If they were found the same fate surely awaited them.

Conditions grew ever worse, Mrs. Dixon in particular was badly affected and became seriously ill. As Rev. Dixon wrote:

"We are much worse off than Mafeking at its worst: and we have no Baden Powell! Comforted greatly by God: and by the thought of the prayers of the Congregations at home. ... There does not seem to be much hope for any of us."

Their only comfort was the fact that the children were safe in Britain; the children in Tai Juan had been slaughtered along with their parents.

By this time there were Boxers in the nearby village. As the site of the cave was known to some non-Christians it was decided that the party should move to another cave some distance away in a less exposed position. For some days they remained there increasingly cold, wet and hungry - by now most of the Christians had fled. But they feared betrayal, and there was no way of escape from their new cave. Once more they made the perilous night journey back to the original cave.

It was more than three weeks since they had left the mission in Hsin Chou; three terrible weeks of occasional searing heat and frequently of cold, relentless rain. For almost all that time they had been forced to hide in dark, damp caves, with hardly any room to move. The native Christians had done their best for them, but they had little to give. Hunger, thirst, arduous journeys from one hiding place to another, the constant fear of discovery, all must have combined to make an ordeal almost impossible to bear. But throughout their tribulations they retained an unshakeable faith in the power of prayer.

Their freedom could not last for ever. By the time Western troops eventually did arrive, the fugitives had been hounded down by the pursuing Boxers. Were they found by chance or were they betrayed? Most probably one of the Christian natives making his way to the cave was followed and either unintentionally or as a result of torture led the pursuers to the cave.

What is certain is that they were discovered. The missionaries possessed shotguns and a revolver and apparently succeeded in driving off the first attack by the Boxers, wounding at least one of their assailants. But the enemy had overwhelming strength in numbers. The eight fugitives were captured and taken back to Hsin Chou where all were put to death. Rev. and Mrs. Dixon, as they had feared, would never see their children again, but their last thoughts would undoubtedly have been with them.

Herbert and Elizabeth Dixon lie in far-off China. But there is in St. David's a second memorial to the Dixons. In Tabernacle Chapel where Elizabeth once worshipped is a plaque bearing the Welsh inscription:

"Er cof am Elizabeth, merch Thomas ac Elizabeth Williams, Clegyr, a Magedig yn yr Eglwys hon. Llofruddiwyd hi a'i phriod, y Parch Herbert Dixon, ar faes Cenhadol China, Awst 1900. 'Dy Ferthyr Di.' "

(In memory of Elizabeth, daughter of Thomas and Elizabeth Williams, Clegyr, reared in this church. She and her husband, Reverend Herbert Dixon, were murdered in the Mission field in China, August, 1900. 'Thine own Martyrs'.)

40. The Memorial to Herbert and Elizabeth Dixon in Tabernacle Chapel.

XVIII; A Famous Rescue

At the time of the Second World War there was another male member of the Williams family apart from Ald. Owen Williams living in St. David's. William Watts Harries Williams, master mariner, known in the family as 'William Inkerman', was the youngest son of John Harries Inkerman Williams, and the only one who lived in St. David's.

His two sisters lived in the houses called New Cross, but William Inkerman and his family lived in Goat Street, opposite the Farmers Arms. Here you would find him most evenings with his cronies entertaining the more gullible of the visitors from 'up the line'. But, no matter how much he had imbibed, the moment the lifeboat maroons were fired he was cool, sober and ready for action.

His bearded face was familiar to a much wider public as that of the 'Welsh Lifeboat Coxswain' of many advertisements for the Royal National Lifeboat Institution. Short, broad-chested, he was almost invariably to be seen wearing a navy blue jersey on which were emblazoned in red the letters RNLI. He was perhaps the most famous of all the fine seamen who have been coxswain of the St. David's lifeboats.

The sea had always been his life. He was one of three of his generation who joined the Merchant Navy; all became master mariners. His eldest brother, Arthur Ernest Inkerman Williams, was one of the last of the 'square rigged' masters, who, as second mate, had been awarded a medal for his part in the rescue of the crew of a brig off Newfoundland. Third of the trio was their cousin Percy Phelps Williams who belonged to the Watts Williams branch of the family.

His first few voyages had been in coastal sloops sailing out of Porthclais. Later the young William Inkerman Williams had been apprenticed for the deep seas in the days of sail, and during that time had sailed around Cape Horn - the ultimate test of sailing ship and crew. Later still he had served with Trinity House and during the First World War on a hospital ship. During the late 1920s he had obtained his first command; his subsequent voyages took him all over the world. But, during the depression, like so many other master mariners he could not find a berth and was forced to return on shore.

In 1936 Captain Watts Williams, 'Skip' as he was affectionately known, was appointed coxswain of the St. David's lifeboat in succession to Ivor Arnold. At the same time a new 46 foot lifeboat arrived to replace the *General Farrell* which, like her coxswain had served the station faithfully for almost a quarter of a century. The new boat was *Civil Service No. 6;* only much later was she given the name *Swn-y-mor*, after the home of the Honorary Secretary, Dr. Joseph Soar, organist of the cathedral.

Soon Britain was at war. In 1940 France was overrun, and Pembrokeshire came within range of enemy bombers. The main targets were Pembroke Dock and the shipping assembled within the Haven which suffered severely. St. David's escaped lightly, only once were bombs dropped nearby, one causing slight damage to the farmhouse at Porthllisky. Alderman Owen Williams was however fortunate on one occasion, having just left a house in City Road, Haverfordwest, when a nearby house suffered a direct hit.

Seldom a night passed however without enemy aircraft being in the area waiting to attack the convoys as they left Milford on their passage up St. George's Channel. Ships were hit, set on fire and sunk. The lifeboat would be launched and Captain Watts Williams and his crew would set out in search of survivors, not knowing if they were to become the next target. Often they brought back seamen wounded, badly burnt or covered in oil; at other times there were no survivors. *Thorold, Port Townsville, Baron Carnegie* .... their names do not appear in the local papers - they were the secret rescues. Only the families and friends of the lifeboatmen were aware of these hazardous wartime rescues.

Even in wartime the sea itself could be the greatest danger of all. On the night of 25th-26th April, 1943, two landing craft on passage from Belfast to Falmouth were overwhelmed at the entrance to Milford Haven. The Angle lifeboat was under repair, and by the time the St. David's lifeboat could fight its way through tumultuous seas to the scene it was in time to rescue only one survivor. Altogether of seventy five men aboard the two ships only three survived - and six seamen from H.M.S. *Rosemary* were lost in a valiant rescue attempt. The lifeboat itself narrowly escaped destruction from a floating mine. The disaster was too great to be kept secret, though details were not released for many years. For his seamanship on this occasion Captain Watts Williams was awarded the bronze medal of the Royal National Lifeboat Institution.

During early March, 1947, Pembrokeshire was swept by one of the worst blizzards in living memory. St. David's was one of many towns and villages which were completely isolated; in spite of strenuous efforts to clear the drifts the main road to Haverfordwest remained blocked for a week, other roads for much longer. Food and fuel began to run out. The lifeboat was despatched to Neyland to pick up supplies and collect the Royal Mail. So it was that *Swn-y-mor* became the last cargo-carrying vessel to enter Porthclais. At the helm was Captain William Watts Williams, descendant of the family whose sloops like *Kitty* and *Favourite Nancy* - ships smaller than the lifeboat - had for many decades brought their cargoes. It was a fitting end to a long tradition.

With the cessation of hostilities there were fewer emergencies; but Captain Watts Williams' finest hour was yet to come. The epic story of the rescue of the crew of the tanker *World Concord* became the lead story on radio and the infant television service, on cinema newsreels and in the daily newspapers. A National Serviceman, a sergeant in the R.A.E.C., stationed in the Suez Canal Zone in Egypt, one of whose duties was to assist in the distribution of daily newspapers flown out to the troops, one morning saw a familiar face on the front page of every paper. The same face was pictured on the front page of the English language Cairo daily, *The Egyptian Gazette;* 'Uncle William Inkerman' was world news.

The *World Concord* was a newly-built, Greek-owned, Liberian-registered oil tanker of some 20,000 tons register. Sailing in ballast from the Mersey to the eastern Mediterranean, in the early hours of Saturday, 27th November, 1954, the giant (for those days) tanker broke in half during a severe gale. Seven of the crew including the master were stranded on the bow section and thirty five on the stern.

Several ships in the vicinity made for the scene but could do nothing immediate to help. Among them was the large aircraft-carrier H.M.S. *Illustrious* aboard which were several helicopters; but neither they nor others from H.M.S. *Goldcrest* at R.N.A.S. Brawdy could lift the sailors off the stricken tanker in the atrocious conditions then prevailing.

It was left to the lifeboats to attempt to rescue the survivors of in effect two wrecks some 15 miles north-northwest of South Bishop. The Fishguard lifeboat was involved with another rescue, leaving only the boats from St. David's and Rosslare available. Shortly before 8.30 a.m. the *Swn-y-mor* was launched to go to the aid of the stern section, while the Rosslare boat was directed to the bow part which was drifting towards the Irish coast.

In command of *Swn-y-mor* was Coxswain William Watts Williams; his crew included two future coxswains; Dai Lewis (second coxswain) and Bill Morris. The remaining crew members were William Rowlands, Howell Roberts and Richard Chisholm together with, in the engine-room, George Jordan and Gwilym Davies.

For over three hours the lifeboat battled through stormy seas towards the stricken tanker. Seen from the deck of the lifeboat she was vast, her metal sides towering high above the *Swn-y-mor* which was pitching violently in the twenty-foot waves. There could be no swift rescue, the men would have to taken off singly; there were thirty five of them, none of whom spoke English.

Captain Watts Williams' plan was to use a Jacob's ladder on the more sheltered starboard side of the tanker to take off the crew one-by-one. With difficulty the strategy was explained to the crew. After a first dummy run the ladder was moved further forward away from the still turning screws of the tanker.

For the second time the lifeboat approached the ladder. This time was for real: there was no room for error. The first terrified sailor had

41. Captain William Watts Harries Williams, 'Skip', at the helm of Marjorie *in the late 1950s off the west coast of Ramsey Island.*

climbed down the ladder as far as he dared. At the critical moment on the crest of a wave the coxswain brought the lifeboat alongside the tanker. The survivor was seized by the lifeboatmen and dragged aboard the *Swn-y-mor*. At the same instant the engines were put astern and the lifeboat backed away.

During the next hour the hazardous manoeuvre was repeated a further thirty four times. It demanded absolute precision on the part of all those on deck, in the engine-room and particularly the coxswain; the slightest error could have led to disaster. Each time the tension grew ever greater; then, at last, the final survivor was aboard *Swn-y-mor*. Even then it was not all over, there was the long haul back to base. For much of the time the lifeboat was out of radio contact and the worst was feared, but at last, as the storm increased still further, the safety of Porth Stinan was reached.

The Rosslare lifeboat was equally successful after an even longer rescue. The famous salvage tug *Turmoil* eventually took the after section in tow and both halves were salvaged and later rejoined. All the crew members of both lifeboats received awards from the R.N.L.I.; Coxswain Watts Williams being awarded the Silver Medal of the Institution. But perhaps the greatest tribute was that paid by the captain of the *Illustrious:*

> "The lifeboat was handled magnificently. It must have required the highest standard of seamanship."

On 7th August, 1955, Queen Elizabeth II and the Duke of Edinburgh visited St. David's, attending morning service at the Cathedral. Among those presented was Captain William Watts Williams. They held a lengthy conversation on his lifeboat experiences during which Her Majesty commented that he reminded her of her grandfather King George V.

The following year, having reached the age of 65, 'Skip' retired from the lifeboat service and was replaced as coxswain by his deputy Dai Lewis of Felin Isaf. But he did not give up the sea. Every summer until his death in January 1961 he would carry visitors in his motor boat *Marjorie* (named after one of his daughters) on trips from Porth Stinan around Ramsey Island to view the coastline and the wildlife which inhabited it. In this time he made many friends. Among them was T. Merfyn Jones, then Chairman of the Wales Gas Board, who owned a cottage on Trefaiddan Moor. He often sailed with 'Skip', and was with him when at the end of summer in 1960 he sailed *Marjorie* back to her winter home of Porthclais for the last time. Let his be the final words:

> "One of our final memories will be of that evening last September when ... we joined him casting off St. Justinian down the Sound and across the calm Porthllysgi still sun drenched, but with a slight northerly that betokened summer's end, making as we know his last mooring in the same Porthclais from which he had first sailed on life's chosen journey."

Genealogical Tables

WATTS of Hayscastle

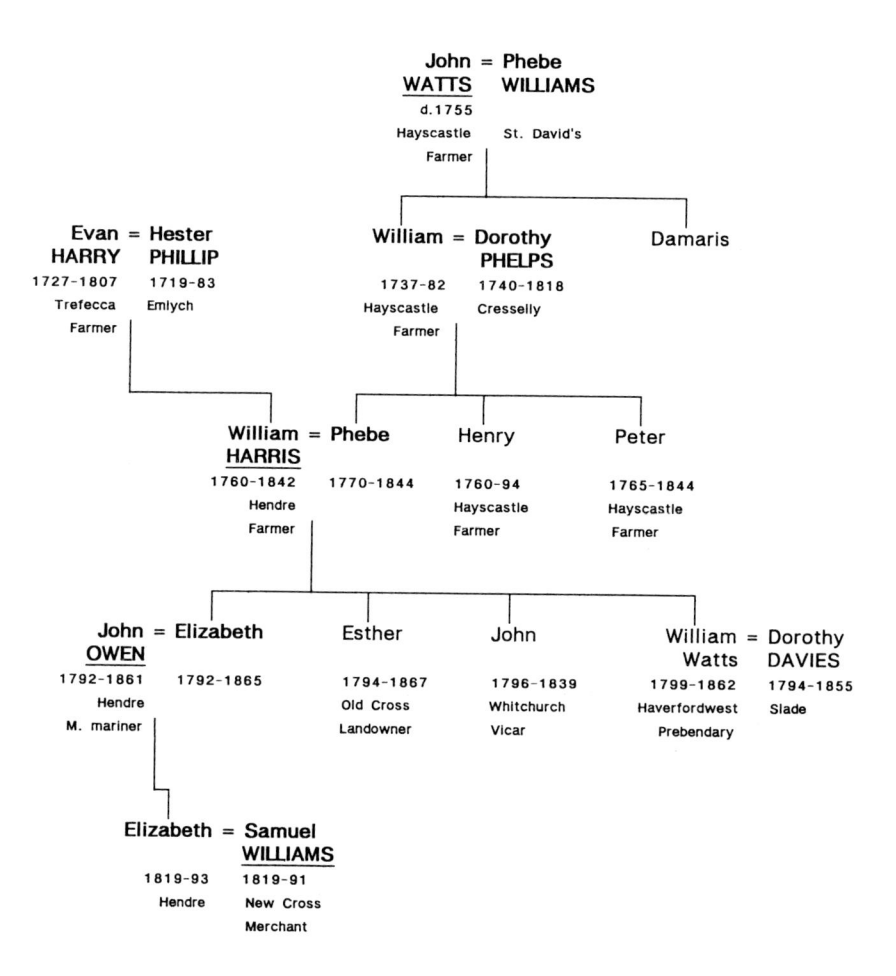

```
                          John    =   Phebe
                          WATTS       WILLIAMS
                          d.1755
                          Hayscastle  St. David's
                          Farmer
```

- Evan HARRY = Hester PHILLIP
  - 1727-1807, 1719-83
  - Trefecca, Emlych
  - Farmer

- William = Dorothy PHELPS
  - 1737-82, 1740-1818
  - Hayscastle, Cresselly
  - Farmer

- Damaris

Children of William & Dorothy:

- William HARRIS = Phebe
  - 1760-1842, 1770-1844
  - Hendre
  - Farmer
- Henry
  - 1760-94
  - Hayscastle
  - Farmer
- Peter
  - 1765-1844
  - Hayscastle
  - Farmer

Children of William HARRIS & Phebe:

- John OWEN = Elizabeth
  - 1792-1861, 1792-1865
  - Hendre
  - M. mariner
- Esther
  - 1794-1867
  - Old Cross
  - Landowner
- John
  - 1796-1839
  - Whitchurch
  - Vicar
- William Watts = Dorothy DAVIES
  - 1799-1862, 1794-1855
  - Haverfordwest, Slade
  - Prebendary

- Elizabeth = Samuel WILLIAMS
  - 1819-93, 1819-91
  - Hendre, New Cross
  - Merchant

HARRIES of Lower Treginnis

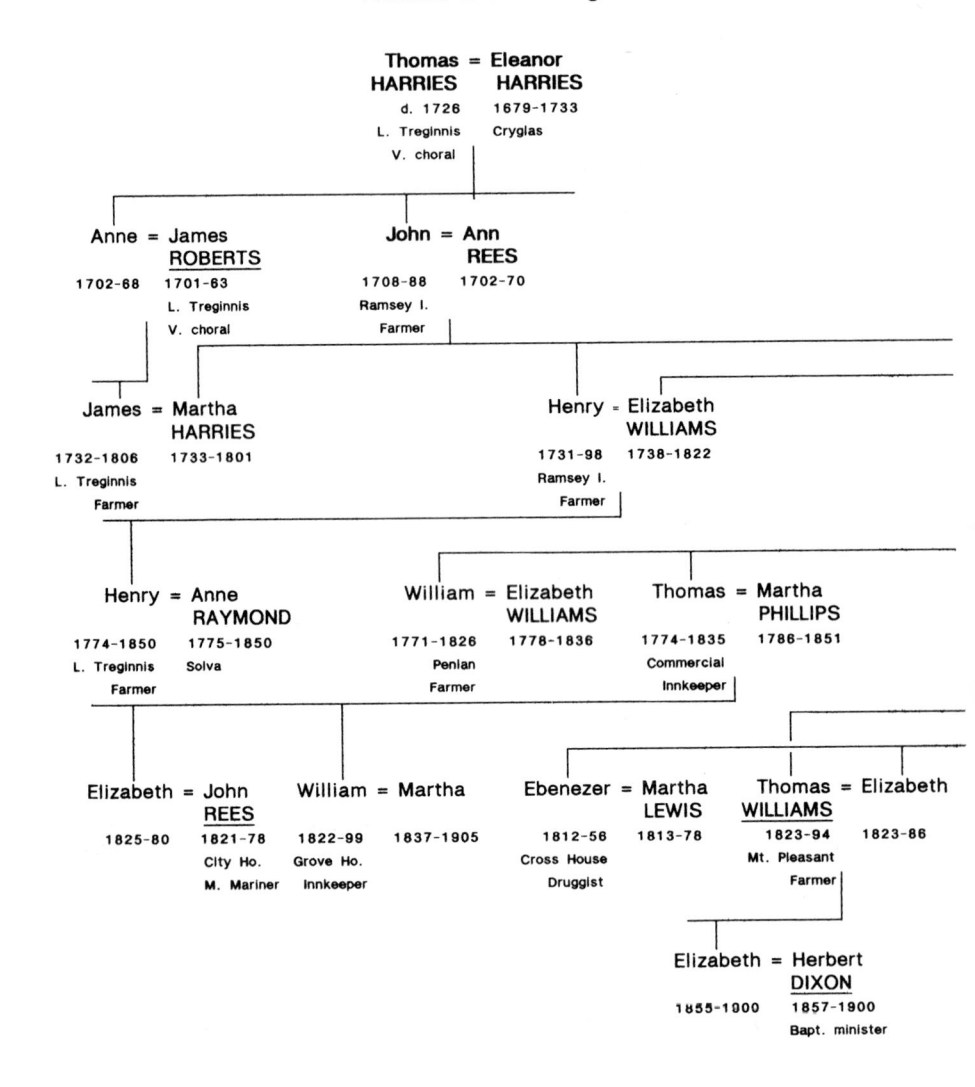

Thomas HARRIES = **Eleanor HARRIES**
d. 1726 — 1679-1733
L. Treginnis — Cryglas
V. choral

- **Anne** 1702-68 = **James ROBERTS** 1701-63, L. Treginnis, V. choral
- **John** 1708-88, Ramsey I., Farmer = **Ann REES** 1702-70

Children:
- **James HARRIES** 1732-1806, L. Treginnis, Farmer = **Martha** 1733-1801
- **Henry** 1731-98, Ramsey I., Farmer = **Elizabeth WILLIAMS** 1738-1822

Next generation:
- **Henry** 1774-1850, L. Treginnis, Farmer = **Anne RAYMOND** 1775-1850, Solva
- **William** 1771-1826, Penlan, Farmer = **Elizabeth WILLIAMS** 1778-1836
- **Thomas** 1774-1835, Commercial Innkeeper = **Martha PHILLIPS** 1786-1851

Next generation:
- **Elizabeth** 1825-80 = **John REES** 1821-78, City Ho., M. Mariner
- **William** 1822-99, Grove Ho., Innkeeper = **Martha** 1837-1905
- **Ebenezer** 1812-56, Cross House, Druggist = **Martha LEWIS** 1813-78
- **Thomas WILLIAMS** 1823-94, Mt. Pleasant, Farmer = **Elizabeth** 1823-86

- **Elizabeth** 1855-1900 = **Herbert DIXON** 1857-1900, Bapt. minister

WILLIAMS of Treginnis

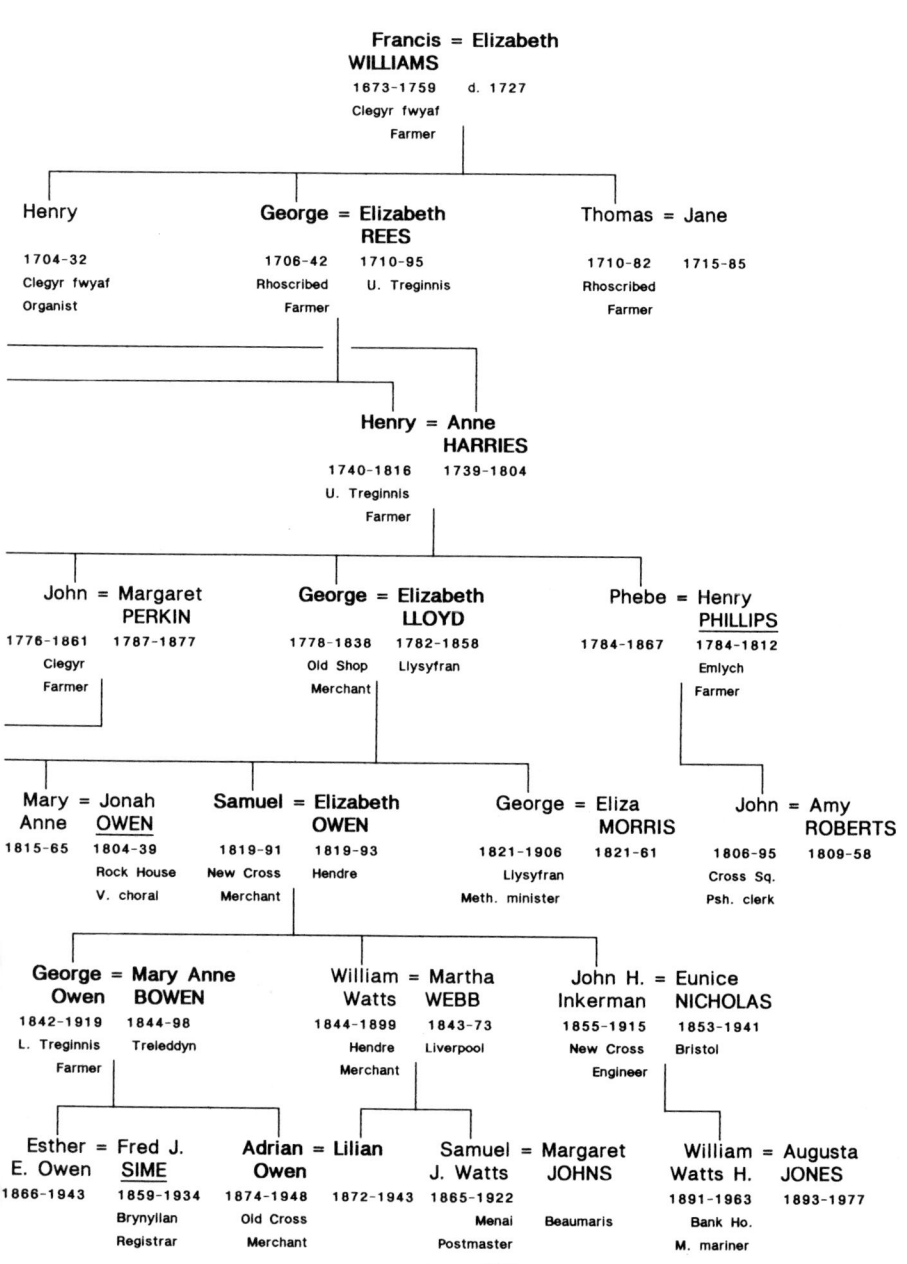

Francis WILLIAMS = **Elizabeth**
1673-1759 d. 1727
Clegyr fwyaf
Farmer

- **Henry**
  1704-32
  Clegyr fwyaf
  Organist

- **George** = **Elizabeth REES**
  1706-42   1710-95
  Rhoscribed U. Treginnis
  Farmer

- **Thomas** = **Jane**
  1710-82   1715-85
  Rhoscribed
  Farmer

Henry = **Anne HARRIES**
1740-1816   1739-1804
U. Treginnis
Farmer

- **John** = **Margaret PERKIN**
  1776-1861   1787-1877
  Clegyr
  Farmer

- **George** = **Elizabeth LLOYD**
  1778-1838   1782-1858
  Old Shop   Llysyfran
  Merchant

- **Phebe** = **Henry PHILLIPS**
  1784-1867   1784-1812
  Emlych
  Farmer

- **Mary Anne** = **Jonah OWEN**
  1815-65   1804-39
  Rock House
  V. choral

- **Samuel** = **Elizabeth OWEN**
  1819-91   1819-93
  Hendre
  Merchant

- **George** = **Eliza MORRIS**
  1821-1906   1821-61
  Llysyfran
  Meth. minister

- **John** = **Amy ROBERTS**
  1806-95   1809-58
  Cross Sq.
  Psh. clerk

- **George Owen** = **Mary Anne BOWEN**
  1842-1919   1844-98
  L. Treginnis Treleddyn
  Farmer

- **William Watts** = **Martha WEBB**
  1844-1899   1843-73
  Hendre   Liverpool
  Merchant

- **John H. Inkerman** = **Eunice NICHOLAS**
  1855-1915   1853-1941
  New Cross   Bristol
  Engineer

- **Esther E. Owen** = **Fred J. SIME**
  1866-1943   1859-1934
  Brynyllan
  Registrar

- **Adrian Owen** = **Lilian**
  1874-1948   1872-1943
  Old Cross
  Merchant

- **Samuel J. Watts** = **Margaret JOHNS**
  1865-1922
  Menai   Beaumaris
  Postmaster

- **William Watts H.** = **Augusta JONES**
  1891-1963   1893-1977
  Bank Ho.
  M. mariner

103

Bibliography

EVANS, Henry: *"Twr-y-Felin" History and Guide to St. David's*, (St. David's, 1923).
FENTON, Richard: *A Tour through Pembrokeshire*, (Brecon, 1811).
GREEN, Francis: Collected Papers, (Haverfordwest Reference Library).
HAMPSON, Desmond G. & MIDDLETON, George W.: *The Story of the St. Davids Lifeboats*, (St. David's, 1974)
HUGHES, J.: 'Cofiant Mr. George Williams', *Y Drysorfa*, (1839).
JAMES, David W.: *St. David's and Dewisland*, (Cardiff, 1981).
JAMES, David W.: 'The Secrets of Dorothy Jordan', *The Pembrokeshire Magazine* No. 37, (Haverfordwest, 1985).
JONES, D. Idwal: *Braslun o Hanes y Tabernacl, Tyddewi*, (St. David's, 1967).
JONES, W. B. & FREEMAN, E. A.: *History & Antiquities of St. David's*, (London, 1856).
LEWIS, Peter: Journal, (1697-1700), (ms, Cardiff Library).
MIDDLETON, George W.: *The Streets of St. Davids*, (St. David's, 1977).
PIGOT: *Commercial Directory of South Wales*, (London, 1830).
THOMAS, John Miles: *Looking Back - A Childhood in Saint Davids Eighty Years Ago*, (Carmarthen, 1977).
WILLIAMS, A. H.: *Wesleyan Methodism in St. Davids - The First 150 Years*, (St. David's, 1968).
WILLIAMS, George: 'Landing of the French at Fishguard 1797', *Pembrokeshire Antiquities*, (Solva, 1897).
WILLIAMS, G. Owen: 'Birds of the District', *The New Illustrated Guide to Historic St. Davids*, (Solva, 1917).
WILLIAMS, Samuel: Letter Books, (N.L.W., Aberystwyth).